OUTSIDE THE BOX WITH
BABAJI

OUTSIDE THE BOX WITH

BABAJI

SONDRA RAY

IMMORTAL RAY
BOOKS

OTHER BOOKS BY SONDRA RAY

- ❖ Rebirthing in the New Age
- ❖ I Deserve Love
- ❖ Loving Relationships I
- ❖ The Only Diet There Is
- ❖ Celebration of Breath
- ❖ Ideal Birth
- ❖ Drinking the Divine
- ❖ Pure Joy
- ❖ Inner Communion
- ❖ How To Be Chic, Fabulous, and Live Forever
- ❖ Interlude With the Gods
- ❖ Loving Relationships II
- ❖ Essays on Creating Sacred Relationships
- ❖ Healing and Holiness
- ❖ Pele's Wish
- ❖ Relationships Treasury
- ❖ Rock Your World with the Divine Mother
- ❖ Liberation Breathing: The Divine Mother's Gift
- ❖ Spiritual intimacy: What You Really Want with a Mate
- ❖ Babaji: My Miraculous Meetings with a Maha Avatar
- ❖ Liberation: Freedom from Your Biggest Block to Pure Joy
- ❖ The New Loving Relationships Book
- ❖ I Deserve Love (2nd Edition)
- ❖ Physical Immortality: How to Overcome Death
- ❖ The Perfection of Babaji
- ❖ Lately I've Been Thinking I
- ❖ Lately I've Been Thinking II
- ❖ The Supermarket for a Meaningful Life

IMMORTAL RAY PRODUCTIONS
301 TINGEY STREET, SE #338
WASHINGTON DC, 20003

Immortal Ray Productions
Nashville   Washington D.C.

Library of Congress Cataloging in Publication Data

Ray, Sondra; Outside the Box With Babaji

I. Self-Help 2. Self-Mastery. 3. Life Wisdom

Cover Design: Markus Ray

Front Cover Photo of Sondra Ray:
Judy Totton Photography of London

Back Cover Painting of Sondra Ray:
Kriss Guenzati Dubini

ISBN 13: Paperback   978-1-950684-17-5
ISBN 13: Hardback   978-1-950684-18-2
ISBN 13: E-Book   978-1-950684-22-9

DEDICATION

To my Guru Babaji, the fountainhead of all my Wisdom—may you always watch over me and bless me with Your inspiration. May You come into my breath and make things clear for me and humanity. I dedicate this book to You and our times we have spent together in this period of the Global Pandemic. Thank you for these words within this book that have come through You. Let me always thrive in Your Presence. Give me the things to say to help myself and others navigate through this Global Revolution that You predicted would be our present challenge. Help me to stay Faithful always to the Forces of Truth, Simplicity, Love and Service that You set in motion—the salvation of each soul in the awakening of their true Self. Help me to awaken fully in this life time. Love, Sondra. Bole Baba Ki Jai!

"GOD'S WILL FOR ME IS PERFECT HAPPINESS."

Lesson # 101 in the Workbook of *A Course in Miracles.*

CONTENTS

FRONTISPIECE —VI

DEDICATION —VII

EPIGRAM —VIII

CONTENTS —IX

FOREWORD BY MARKUS RAY —XV

INTRODUCTION —XX

OUTSIDE THE BOX WITH BABAJI —1

CHAPTER 1 ~
OVERCOMING OUR EGO —2

CHAPTER 2 ~
OVERCOMING FEAR —6

CHAPTER 3 ~
OVERCOMING GUILT —28

CHAPTER 4 ~
OVERCOMING BAD HABITS
AND ADDICTIONS —40

CHAPTER 5 ~
OVERCOMING ANGER —48

CHAPTER 6 ~
OVERCOMING THE EGO —53

CHAPTER 7 ~
OVERCOMING TENSION —57

CHAPTER 8 ~
OVERCOMING WORRY –59

CHAPTER 9 ~
OVERCOMING SUFFERING –62

CHAPTER 10 ~
OVERCOMING GRIEF –69

CHAPTER 11 ~
LETTING GO –71

CHAPTER 12 ~
ACHIEVING RELAXATION –79

CHAPTER 13 ~
HAVING SAFETY –81

CHAPTER 14 ~ HEALING –83

CHAPTER 15 ~ GOD –102

CHAPTER 16 ~
WRITING THE MASTER –105

CHAPTER 17 ~ ADVANCING –107

CHAPTER 18 ~ GETTING STRONGER –108

CHAPTER 19 ~ FUTURE –109

CHAPTER 20 ~ PERFECTION –112

CHAPTER 21 ~ FEELING GOOD –117

CHAPTER 22 ~ HAVING FUN –126

CHAPTER 23 ~ SEX –128

CHAPTER 24 ~ LOVE –132

CHAPTER 25 ~
RELATIONSHIPS –133

CHAPTER 26 ~
REASONS PEOPLE "SETTLE FOR LESS" IN A
RELATIONSHIP –136

CHAPTER 27 ~
RECIPE FOR GREAT RELATIONSHIPS –138

CHAPTER 28 ~ PROSPERITY –141

CHAPTER 29 ~ PRAYER –144

CHAPTER 30 ~ JOY –148

CHAPTER 31 ~ CLARITY –157

CHAPTER 32 ~
PHYSICAL IMMORTALITY –159

CHAPTER 33 ~ ATONEMENT –162

CHAPTER 34 ~ FAITH –164

CHAPTER 35 ~ TRUTH –174

CHAPTER 36 ~ WHO WE ARE –175

CHAPTER 37 ~ THE HOLY SPIRIT –178

CHAPTER 38 ~ THE DREAM TEAM –180

CHAPTER 39 ~ SPIRITUAL PRACTICE –183

CHAPTER 40 ~ FASTING –184

CHAPTER 41 ~ GRATITUDE –186

CHAPTER 42 ~ SURRENDER –187

CHAPTER 43 ~ MIRACLES –193

PART II: THE DIVINE MOTHER –194

CHAPTER 44 ~ THE DIVINE MOTHER –196

CHAPTER 45 ~ WHO IS BABAJI? –203

CHAPTER 46 ~ LIBERATION BREATHING –207

CHAPTER 47 ~ MANTRA BREATHING –215

CHAPTER 48 ~ ADDITIONS –233

CHAPTER 49 ~ AFFIRMATIONS –241

AN INVITATION FROM SONDRA RAY,
"THE MOTHER OF REBIRTHING" –253

ABOUT THE AUTHOR –255
OTHER RESOURCES –258
BOOKS BY SONDRA RAY & MARKUS RAY –260

FOREWORD

Intertwined in life, and equally intertwined in all creative actions, Sondra Ray and I work together.

Outside the Box with Babaji is her baby, but I am the one who holds the space for the delivery of this sacred child.

As much as I cannot interfere with the birthing process, I sit attentively on the sidelines allowing the ease of the delivery to take place.

A home must be prepared to receive this new Being—a birth soon here.

That is my job as the midwife of this glorious moment of new Life coming upon our planet.

I sit in the corner, weaving the proper outfit to clothe these words of an immaculate order of things.

We decided on a font, a book size, a layout, a general feel of this baby yet to come. That's also my job in the process.

I am the book designer here.

What we are delivering must have these conditions of birth just right. The baby about to come into this world from the nine months of gestation is at hand.

That is the time Sondra Ray has been jotting down these "news feeds" from Babaji in her weekly meditations with Him. It's their "baby together."

Babaji and Sondra Ray go back many lifetimes. Seven to be exact. She has stood with Him many times "outside the box."

Here she is again, standing again with Babaji. Lucky for you.

This is a different kind of book, requiring a different kind of reading. Because it is a different kind of message.

Babaji is a Maha Avatar. Perhaps you have never met such a Being. Meeting Him would be like meeting Jesus—off the charts.

Sondra met Him numerous times in this lifetime. And still does in her etheric connections with Him in meditation.

All of this book is her dialogue with Him. It is "outside the box" of normal thinking.

It is "outside the box" of limitations that we commonly impose on ourselves.

Babaji and Sondra Ray want to take you and me "outside the box" with them.

These words are distilled nectar that can do that. They can nourish us with the Joy of a New Being in our midst.

That New Being is our Higher Self. You and I can receive this Child of Holiness within us.

We will be "rebirthed" by this book. Sondra Ray is the "Mother of Rebirthing," so this is apropos to happen.

Give yourself a lot of space to soak this book in. Read it slower than slow. One or two lines merit sustained attention.

You will find yourself going into an "altered state."

What would that be, you must wonder?

You will still be you. Yet the *You* that you will be, during and after reading this book, will be someone you yearned to meet "on the road to Damascus."

You will meet your True Self. Love will engulf you beyond your imaginings. You will find yourself "Outside the Box with Babaji" in the glory of your own Pure Joy.

Markus Ray

INTRODUCTION

I started this book with my Master, Babaji, during the Pandemic. Every week I would give myself a Liberation Breathing session and ask Him to be there. I jotted down what I heard. It is my supreme honor to be able to share all this with you.

The first part is deep and may bring up subconscious material for you to clear. If you need any support for that, contact us for a Liberation Breathing session at bit.ly/LBSession.

The next part came at the end of the pandemic, and this part will make you feel good. The book gets easier and more wonderful as you go along. You will feel higher and higher as you keep reading!

Towards the end I describe for you Liberation Breathing, and, "What is Mantra Breathing?" I invite you to try it.

The last part is my attempt to explain who is Babaji and who is the Divine Mother. Their Love is available for you.

I certainly hope you make your Divine Connection with Them and ENJOY yourself reading this.

Sondra Ray

How to Read this book —

Try to avoid reading this book just like you would read an ordinary book. Reading a spiritual book for bringing transformation inside you is an art. Read it very, very slowly, and contemplate the meaning of each statement. Let the words touch you. Don't be in a hurry. You want to be able to implement the information in real life. Every time you read it again and again, you will find a deeper meaning. Every reading should bring some transformation in you. My goal is that you experience more peace, more joy, more healing, and certainly more wisdom. I also want it to prepare you for what Babaji calls the *Kranti.* By that He meant "global revolution." We are just at the beginning of the Kranti. You are going to need support from a Master to navigate through it.

Also, I am thrilled to introduce Babaji to you in this way.

Try to consciously love yourself for reading this book. Let go of all judgements of yourself.

The first part of the book is kind of a cleansing. If ever you feel that it brings up too much in you, just take a breath and relax. You can contact us for a Liberation Breathing private session, and/or attend my readings of *Outside the Box with Babaji*, which are presented while people are lying down breathing. Go here to see the next one: bit.ly/Ray-Talks

You will feel better and better as you keep reading. This is because you will have cleared things so that you will be able to enjoy the later parts of the book, which are higher thoughts that will bring you joy.

The book is the result of my personal weekly Liberation Breathing Sessions I practiced during the Pandemic. I was looking for answers for myself and the world, and this is what came through. It was not like I left my body and Babaji took me over. It was more like I downloaded these thoughts, many of which were for me—but also for mankind in general. Since I was lying down breathing at the time, I received these ideas in my own voice in my head, so I jotted them down on cards each week. That is how I got the idea people should lie down and breathe when I am reading this book to the public on some Sundays. Anyone can come. You can participate in **RAY TALKS™** Sunday at 1:00 PM, Eastern USA time over Zoom. Either Markus gives a talk on ACIM, or I give a talk from *Outside the Box with Babaji.*

Part Two of this book is dedicated to the Divine Mother. Babaji is the one who led me back to Her, and He said Himself, "I leave everything in the hands of the Divine Mother," when He consciously left his body on February 14, 1984. Recently, while giving myself Breathwork sessions, I started receiving affirmations that felt really good to me. I was hearing these affirmations in my head. I had no idea if they were from me or Babaji, but it did not matter since we are always on a "Joint Project." You can borrow them from me. I am willing to share this very intimate part of my mind because I can only assume these thoughts will also benefit you as they have done for me.

I am pretty sure you will want to go into a deeper relationship with Babaji after reading this book. Then, I would refer you to also read our other books on Babaji:

Babaji: My Miraculous Meetings with a Maha Avatar

&

The Perfection of Babaji

We would also hope you come to India with us for The Divine Mother Festival at Babaji's Ashram. Until the pandemic we went every year in the Spring. This year (2022) we went back, since India has eased its travel restrictions. The link for that trip is always: bit.ly/IQRay

Bole Baba Ki Jai, we say!

OUTSIDE THE BOX WITH
BABAJI

OVERCOMING OUR EGO

People are not dealing with their "negative mental mass." What is that?

- ❖ All negativity
- ❖ All guilt
- ❖ All fear
- ❖ All anger
- ❖ All resistance
- ❖ All rebellion
- ❖ All unwillingness
- ❖ All death-urge
- ❖ All lack
- ❖ All limitation
- ❖ All faithlessness
- ❖ All depression

The Five "Biggies"

1. Birth Trauma
2. Specific Negative Thoughts
3. Parental Disapproval Syndrome
4. Unconscious Death-Urge
5. Other Lifetimes

All this is our ego. What's our "case?"

It is our personal shadow, our family shadow, our religious shadow and all of the above. We must get beyond our "case" because when it is "up," we are not available for God.

One has to overcome the belief in separation.

One has to overcome one's worst thought about oneself, which we call a "personal lie."

One has to overcome fear, guilt and anger.

One has to overcome always focusing on the problem instead of the solution, or on "what's not working" instead of "what is working!"

One has to overcome limited thinking and self-sabotage.

One has to overcome addictions and negative behaviors.

One has to overcome thinking one knows it all.

One has to overcome doubting there is a Force greater than our strength that can help us.

One has to overcome the belief that the ego is all there is!

OVERCOMING FEAR

We think fear is real. We are using fear to replace love. We do not need fear if we place the future in the hands of God. Are we willing to do that? That would be the solution to all fear. But we would have to learn to trust the Unknown. The Unknown is God. The Unknown is therefore safe. But we believe that the Unknown is somehow unsafe. We think that the Unknown might be dangerous. The Unknown, however is actually where the safety is. We have to trust this.

There is nothing to fear.
Lesson 48 in ACIM

Fear is not justified in any form.   Lesson 240 in ACIM

All fear is past and only love is here. Lesson #293 in ACIM

I gladly make the sacrifice of fear.   Lesson 323 in ACIM

People fear that something bad will happen; but they even have fear that something really good will happen. For example, people have fear of miracles— that is because miracles are a shock to one's belief system. If we want a miracle, we have to pray for release of the fear of the miracle first, before it can happen.

If we had no fear at all, we would not attract anything dangerous.

Think about that. We think something dangerous might happen, so this gives us fear. But fear attracts danger. We think we have fear because of danger; but we really have a sense of danger because of fear. Fear comes before the danger.

What is our fear of giving up fear? We should ask ourselves this question. The answer will probably be that we would be in ecstasy.

Ecstasy is not scary; it is just unfamiliar. How do we correct fear?

a. We must be willing to find the thought causing the fear.
b. We must be willing to give that thought up.
c. We then must turn it over to the Holy Spirit.

When there is no more fear, there is no more pain.

We are totally safe without fear. The Higher Self has no fear. We are really only our Higher Self.

Fear and happiness cannot occupy the same space.

To be symptomless, we have to give up all fear.

Fear causes symptoms in the body. Some say they do not have any symptoms; but that does not mean they still don't have fear. The fear is suppressed in the subconscious mind; therefore, they might not be aware of it. Someday it is sure to come up. Unfortunately, it often shows up as a symptom. A person would be almost too scared to FEEL that fear so it comes out as a symptom instead.

I am saying that most people don't process their fear because they think it is too scary to feel the fear. We are fortunate to have Liberation Breathing to breathe out any fear. Any discomfort doing this in a session is temporary.

The guru will bring up all unconscious fears to be released, and this is good. There is infinite value in having a guru.

We are not so unhappy because we have symptoms. We are unhappy because of the fear. Fear wipes out our happiness.

Most people don't process their fear because it is usually very suppressed. But as we said, we have the Breathwork to breathe out any fear. Any discomfort doing this in a session is temporary.

Discomfort brings up fear; and fear brings up discomfort. Sometimes in A Liberation Breathing Session you have to go through feeling the discomfort caused by

We are totally
safe without
fear.

The Higher Self
has no fear.

We are really
ONLY our
Higher Self.

fear—until you breathe it out. It is always worth it to go through that.

An inner state of *no fear* brings about total relaxation.

People are afraid to go to the next level; but it is going to feel like the most natural thing in the world. When we get there, we are going to wonder why we had fear and why we hesitated; as it will feel good.

Many older people have this very deep subconscious fear that they will get a condition in their body that they could not get over or get rid of. Younger people have different fears—like, "Will I ever find my perfect mate, job, career, house, sense of accomplishment, etc." When it comes to healing a condition in our body, we have to trust that all things are possible. We can overcome any condition. Since we made up the condition with our mind, we can *unmake* it.

We need to keep saying: "All fear is gone." If we keep saying that, it cannot exist. That also means we are ready to let go of symptoms which were caused by the fear.

What we fear is total enlightenment. Why? Because one is still afraid of the Unknown. However, enlightenment will only bring joy. It is painless. It releases pain. It is miraculous. It is the state of being you are craving. It is your natural God-given state.

People have fear of giving up fear! This is crazy; but the ego has us tricked into thinking that if we give it up, something terrible will happen. **The ego is fear.**

We need to say that we offer up to the Holy Spirit our stubborn refusal to give up fear.

There is no reason to have fear of being great. Only good things will happen to us if we keep offering up our ego for release. Without fear, we are as great as God created us to be.

We should not try to *master fear*. That just gives it more power. The answer is to replace it with God's perfect love. Grace and mercy can remove the fear without us doing anything.
Sometimes one's fear feels like a chain around the neck. One should write down one's three worst fears and then breathe them out in a Liberation Breathing session.

In case we are feeling the fear and it is really scary, it helps to think as hard as possible about someone who really loves us. Then we also can learn to do wet rebirthing in warm water and this truly helps.

Breathing out fear is actually fun. Every time we let go of fear, it feels good.

Let's say we have fear that we are not going to make it. The answer is to stay in present time where we are making it this minute. Then remember to place the future in the hands of God.

By now we see that letting go of fear is a top priority. Why is it a slow process to let go of fear? That is because:

a. It is an addiction
b. People are terrified of sudden healings
c. People make fear real

It would be a faster process if we just stepped into believing that there is no fear. People don't do that because they *feel* the pain or whatever caused by the fear and then they make it real.

One can simply de-materialize fear. Say this, "Fear no longer exists in my reality."

Fear will end when we end it. No fear equals more joy. Anything that is not wonderful is fear because there are only two possible emotions: Love or Fear.
Fear tightens everything up in the body, stops the flow of life and makes us weak.

We have to forgive ourselves for making fear real. God did not make fear. Letting go of fear feels good. One can always make up more fear; but why do that?

By removing fears, the joy of God can spring up.

What we thought were fears were really illusions. An illusion is like a mirage—it is not really there, even though it appears to be.

Worry is just indulging in fear. We cannot stop worrying until we let go of the fear causing it. Worry is a waste of time. Practice giving up worry.

Perfect love casts out fear. Fear does not really exist, because really only perfect love exists. We should say, *"I AM the perfect love of God."*

We have the power to change every fear thought for a happy thought of love. We want to get to the point where we are not worried or alarmed about anything.

> *Perfect love casts out fear.*
> *If fear exists,*
> *Then there is not perfect love.*

But,

Only perfect love exists.
If there is fear,
It produces a state that does not
exist.

(ACIM; Text; Chapter 1; Section iv)

The reason we don't let the Holy Spirit take all of our fear is because it is an addiction and we think it would be too easy if the Holy Spirit just took it from us. But it is right to have it easy. God wants us to have it easy.

Everything that is not working in our life is more or less due to fear. We might think we don't have any fear and yet, if we look at what is not working in our life, we will see there is fear.
Fear makes everything shrink and contract (but Love is expansion).

Fear is a huge addiction. We hang on to it and it attracts all kinds of bad things like illnesses. The fear feels like a "thing" in our body and that thing becomes a symptom or a disease.

Obviously, we will have more miracles when we give up fear. Fear blocks the miraculous from happening in our life.

Embracing our Real Self eliminates fear. Our Real Self has faith in the miraculous.

If we take away the fear, faith will come in. We need to ask the Holy Spirit to take all of our fear so we can experience 100% faith.

Holy Spirit, help me to see that fear is not real.

Help me to deny fear.

Since the separation is not real, therefore, fear is not real.

Important: Fear brings in negative things. When we have a lot of fear, we also make a lot of mistakes.

When we agree with fear, we are giving what we fear the right to come into possibility. Don't come into agreement with fear! A Loving Force protects us and gives us the possibilities of more Peace and Joy!

Say this Prayer: *Holy Spirit, help me see that fear is not real. Help me to deny fear. Since the separation is not real, therefore fear is not real.*

When fear is gone, one expands greatly. We must replace fear with faith.

We must allow the love of the Holy Spirit to remove our fear.

The way out of huge fear:

1. Note the negative thought causing the fear and change it.
2. Get that God is perfect love, and you are perfect love, and in that there is no fear.
3. Forgive yourself for making up the fear in the first place.
4. Say to the Holy Spirit, "I release my stubborn refusal to give up fear and I allow You to help."
5. Accept the love of the Masters which will melt the fear.
6. Get that fear is an illusion.
7. Breathe out the imagined fear in a Liberation Breathing Session.

Having fear is the same as saying, "I do not trust God."

Fear of the future is a common addiction.

When one moves forward or breaks through to something higher, or goes to the next level, a fear of the future could accompany this. Watch out for that. One has to remind oneself that one can move ahead and not have a fear of the future. "I place the future in the hands of God." (ACIM; Lesson #194)

When feeling a lot of fear, one should say, " I allow God's perfect love to cast out this fear."

When feeling fear, one must come up with a solution that erases the fear. The solution is always our Divine Connec-tion. This is where spiritual practices are essential, because they give us the certainty we need to trust our own Energy is enough to solve any problem, including overcoming an addiction.

Babaji has always told me that the recitation of "Om Namah Shivay" is one of the most powerful spiritual practices anybody can do. Anyone can do it, any time. Just get a set of 108 mala beads, the simple kind with wooden beads, and say "Om Namah Shivay" 108 times a day. Apply it to your "addiction." Think of the mantra "burning away your desire" for the thing you are addicted to in the moment. Babaji will come through for you if you are sincere and not just faking it. See what happens.

Most people never process their fear. First of all, they may not even be in touch with it, as it is usually suppressed. Second of all, it is usually too scary to feel it. The problem is then, that it will eventually lead to trouble, pains, and or illnesses.

Releasing fear feels great; however, the ego is going to try to get us to hang on to the fear.

We need to ask for God's perfect love to cast out our fear.

Fear feels real because of the intensity it stirs up in the body. But it feels intense because we made it real in the first place. Holding on to fear makes it only *seem* more real; but we are holding on to it because we *think* it is real. There is a higher reality that transcends our ego's thinking. Fear is definitely a sign the ego is hanging on to control.

Above all, we need to give up fear of giving up fear!

Try this: *Whatever is in me that needs to happen to safely release all my fear, happens now! The Holy Spirit now shows me how to STOP making fear real. I now have God's Perfect Love!*

Only *perfect love* is real—so how could anything unlike love (such as fear) even exist? The mantra is *God's perfect love*, therefore, it can wipe out fear. Letting go of fear makes one a lot sharper! Life without fear = Heaven on earth.

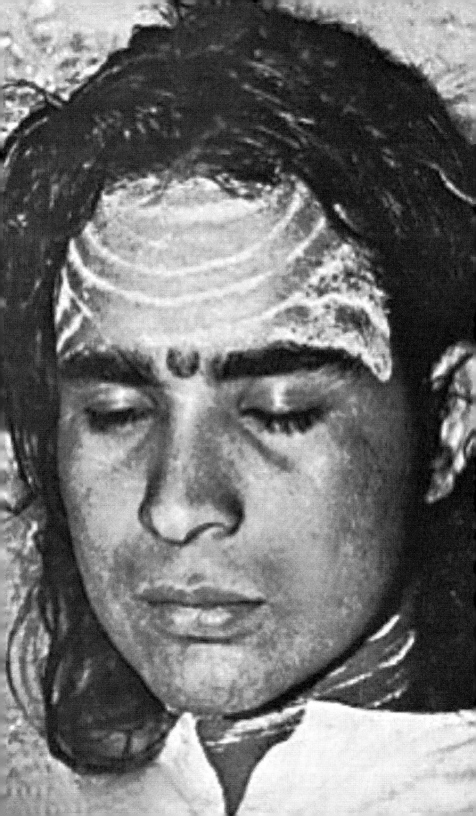

OVERCOMING GUILT

Guilt demands punishment and makes us suffer.

Guilt induces fear of retaliation and condemnation.

- ❖ We all have past life guilt / birth trauma guilt (hurting our mother at birth).
- ❖ We all have some religious guilt (thinking we were born sinners). Even if we are atheists, we still carry some guilt.

❖ We all have some guilt about things we did that we think were bad.

The separation is our original guilt. The ego is the symbol of guilt. We thought we were separate from the Life Force (God) but it's impossible to be separate from our Source of Life.

While guilt is attractive the mind and body will suffer.

The belief in sin causes tremendous guilt and is a request for death. The ego tells us that we deserve death.

Love and guilt cannot co-exist. Peace and guilt cannot co-exist.

The attraction of guilt produces fear of love.

Guilt is not merely not of God, it is an attack on God.

Guilt has obscured the Father to us, and is driving us insane. Guilt hides our Higher Self (Christ) from our sight.

To the ego, there is no escape from guilt. It will tell us that if we DARE think we are innocent, then we are really guilty!

Guilt makes us more attracted to behavior that will make us feel guilty. This feeling makes us do more bad things in the future.

Those who hold grievances will suffer guilt. If we yield to guilt, we are deciding against happiness.

It is up to us if we want to feel guilty. God sees only our innocence.

To heal ourselves, we have to know we are innocent. Otherwise, we will keep the condition as a punishment for guilt. Innocence can ward off any disease.

If we try to go "big time" without clearing our guilt, we could crash and burn out there. If we really expand our life and become a huge figure without clearing guilt, the punishment we create could be greater. We could fall further, in other words.

Guilt makes us blind. While we have one spot of guilt, we will not see the light.

The belief in guilt leads to a belief in hell. The glitter of guilt we lay on our bodies will kill us. Because of guilt, we are addicted to feeling bad. We are addicted to the ego and creating hell for ourselves, and eventually death.

Guilt can manifest as psychosomatic diseases, accident proneness, and suicidal behavior.

One way we punish ourselves for guilt is to create pain and tension.

When we give up guilt and fear, we are automatically relaxed.

The reason we do things that make us feel guilty or feel like rebelling is so that we can have a false sense of autonomy, which promotes separation from God.

People have been punishing them-selves in so many ways because they thought they were *bad* in past lives. But *God says this: There is nothing bad in you that is real. Why do you punish yourselves for something that does not even exist?*

God says this:

There is nothing bad in you that is real.

Why do you punish yourselves for something that does not even exist?

Our Higher Self has no guilt. We *are* our Higher Self.

But what if one has a "guilt attack?" Maybe something was done wrongly. It feels bad. One might then get a headache or some other ailment. The headache makes one feel like this guilt is really real. And yet, if a person does not make the guilt real, then there would be no headache.

Guilt is a way of holding the past in our mind. Regret and guilt result from equating the present self with the former self.

Excessive guilt can be a form of egotism in which the self becomes blown up, exaggerated and the "hero" of the tragedy—the negativity feeds the ego.

Wallowing in guilt is an indulgence. The error is inflated instead of relinquishing it to a Higher Power.

One has to **decide** if one is going to cling to it and get the "juice," or give it up. If one does not decide, no healing can occur.

Trying to get rid of guilt with one's own mind probably won't work. If one focuses on the guilt, it will then get worse. What to do? We need to turn it over to the Holy Spirit. But that seems too easy, so most people won't even do that. This is the time for spiritual practice.

Then one should keep on praying to the Holy Spirit for help in **not** making the guilt real. One's Real Self is the perfect love of God and perfect innocence. There is no guilt in that, so this is why guilt does not exist in reality. (This teaching is hard to get and one should not beat oneself up if it takes quite some time to really grok it.)

Unless we are guiltless, we cannot know God. And the only way to escape pain is guiltlessness. We are meant to have certainty of our God Self, free of pain.

We project guilt to get rid of it; but that is only concealing it. If we displace it onto others, the Holy Spirit cannot help us with it.

We must also look upon our brother as guiltless.

Do we want to escape from guilt? Then we must say, "I am as God Created me. His Son can suffer nothing, and I am His Son." (ACIM; Workbook; Lesson #110) The "Answer" is the accepting of the Atonement.   When we have really accepted it, there will be no guilt in us.

The Holy Spirit seeks to remove all guilt from our mind so that we may remember our Father. By invitation, the Holy Spirit transforms our mind by the healing power of grace.

Our holiness is our salvation, which is the end of guilt. The guiltless mind cannot suffer.

Recovery may include: confession / forgiveness / penance / renewal of spiritual principles / good works / selfless service / & humanitarian efforts.

We have to see the difference between "error" and "sin." Error is just a mistake that can be corrected. "Sin" has with it the notion that we are inherently "bad" and we deserve punishment. Which would you rather have—a mistake that can be corrected or a sin that demands punishment because of our "guilt?" The ego will always choose the latter. It is addicted to guilt. Our Higher Self will choose correction and restoration of our *original innocence.*

Markus and I have a great affirmation that we say to ourselves the moment we notice we have made a mistake. It goes something like this:

Even though I made a mistake, I still completely love and accept myself.

This saves us from all unnecessary self-punishment because of any associated guilt.

What salvation is—is the escape from all guilt!

OVERCOMING BAD HABITS & ADDICTIONS

Guilt causes us to do things that are not good for us. When we do *that thing*, we feel the guilt. Example: a gambler is punishing himself for his guilt by losing. Then this becomes an addiction.

When we indulge in the addiction, we feel more guilt. We have to forgive ourselves and try again to let it go. But guilt adds weight to the situation and it gets harder and harder to give up the addiction.

At first the addiction might make us feel good; but pretty soon we will feel bad about it and more guilty. We get so stuck in guilt that we cannot let it go. If we add guilt for *not* giving up the addiction (which was caused by guilt) now we have a double whammy and we get more stuck.

The addiction makes us weak, and then we miss the glory of feeling really strong. When we are finally ready to give up an addiction, we will set up the circumstances for the decision to work.

When one's guilt is no longer tolerable, one will give up the habit. We have to finally face how much the addiction is damaging us.

One will not miss the addiction after giving it up, if one puts God in that place instead.

One can replace the celebration one felt from the addiction (such as excessive drinking) by thinking every-thing is a celebration.

One should forgive oneself for taking so long to get over it.

Commit to this: From now on we only do what is good for us. One would think one would not have to say that; however, we continue to indulge in bad habits and addictions.

One may decide to quit many times but cannot. It helps to make the **decision** out loud with a witness.

We are addicted to our personal lie (our most negative thought about ourself). It is very deceptive, crafty and cunning. People wrestle with it their whole lives. It may be brought in from a past life. We more completely explain the subject of personal lies in our book:

Liberation: Freedom from Your Biggest Block to Pure Joy : bit.ly/LibRay

Let's say one's personal lie is I AM BAD. Then one might have a fear of being good and a fear of not being good. Let's say one's personal lie is I AM NOT PERFECT. Then one could have a fear of being perfect and a fear of not being perfect. This vacillation keeps one stuck in the personal lie.

It seems almost easier to give up an addiction to a substance than to a thought pattern that is an addiction. You can remove the substance totally and easily and therefore you don't take it. But for a thought pattern that is an addiction, what does one do? Here is where you must become the Christ. Start saying, "I am the Christ."

When stopping an addiction, the withdrawals will be much less if one can forgive oneself totally for having had the addiction.

Sometimes being addicted to a pattern is worse than to a substance. If we are totally stuck in some fear, guilt or anger with an addictive pattern, it is like being addicted to Hell. One has to face that. One has to confess that.

When one lets go of enough fear, the opposite of the addiction can start to come forth. One has to admit that one was wrong. One has to admit that one has tried to replace God with the ego. One has been in competition with God, and trying to *kill God.*

God wills that we be happy. Therefore, the will of this Force which created the Universe is at our disposal to eliminate what keeps us from happiness— addictions being one of these things. Would we take advantage of that powerful Force? Surely it could help us to overcome an addiction if we are in earnest, and truly want to give it up.

We have a step in the undoing process that goes like this: "I give up my stubborn refusal to let this thought (or pattern, or addiction) go." It is usually our own stubborn refusal that blocks us from healing an addiction.

When we give up our "stubborn refusal," the Holy Spirit can help us in overcoming any addiction.

We also need to give up our "payoff" for keeping the addiction. There is some neurotic benefit we get out of the whole thing. We could be feeding an addiction to *stay small* and not utilize our full potential. Maybe we have a fear of putting ourself "out there." The addiction may justify us not facing our fear.

When we are ready to give up our "payoff," we are also ready to let the addiction go. The Holy Spirit can help us in releasing both the payoffs and the addiction simultaneously.

OVERCOMING ANGER

Sometimes we get angry that we have a symptom in our body—especially if it does not go away. The problem is that the anger keeps it more stuck and in place.

Anger is very bad for us. It ruins our health. It pushes people away. It makes us vibrate at a very low level. It can also destroy the former spiritual work we have done on ourself.

We cannot even get by with irritation. Under irritation is a veil of hate. ACIM says anger is *never justified*.

When we are angry, we cannot hear God.

GAF (Guilt, Anger & Fear) is where everyone is stuck.

It is a good idea to have the thought, "I am no longer upset by anything."

Letting go of anger opens us up to all the good things.

Complaining makes us sick and is unfair to others who have to listen to us. Let's not indulge in derogatory talk about anything or anyone, or our mind will become impure.

Anger has fear attached to it. That is because it is a defense, and defenses attract attack. Then, when we have anger we will unconsciously fear attack.

When we totally let go of anger, the fun is unlimited.

Yelling is very hateful and hurtful. Why do it? Do you like to hear someone who is angry? Obviously not. People tune you out when you are angry.

We cannot let in God's love when we are angry. We block it. We have free will to keep God out by keeping our anger. God is right there but cannot penetrate us when we keep our anger.

We "set up" things not to work so that we can stay angry! This is super important to understand.

If we "keep" our anger, we will constantly make up scenarios that are upsetting so we can feel the anger. Guilt demands punishment, just like anger demands an upset.

Keeping anger will prevent one's diet from working!

Fear and anger are like knotted nets holding everything stuck in an undesirable place.

Say this: "I trade in my anger for Joy."

We cannot let in God's love when we are angry. We block it. We have free will to keep God out by keeping our anger. God is right there but cannot penetrate us when we keep our anger.

OVERCOMING THE EGO

One needs to say the following: "I give up the part of my ego that is in competition with God. I give up the part of it that wants to *be* God. I give up the part that wants to replace God. I call in the Dream Team (Babaji, The Divine Mother, and Jesus of *A Course in Miracles*), and I call in Archangel Michael to help me with this."

We must give up the part of our ego that wants to create an upset.

The ego has not only manifested the negative condition, it wants us to stay upset about the condition—on top of having it! It's a double whammy!

We must say: I give up the part of my mind (ego) that wants to keep the bad condition going—the part of me that is attracted to pain.

The ego pattern is actually taking up space in one's mind/body which is causing the condition. The ego is taking on a form (pain, symptoms or disease). When we let it go, the light comes back in.

We don't want to look at or face the part of us (ego) that wants to kill God. Sickness is an attempt to kill God!

We must turn over the part of our ego that does not want to be turned over!

We must say:

I give up the part of my mind (ego) that wants to keep the bad condition going— the part of me that is attracted to pain.

The ego will tell us that the situation is hopeless.

We must replace our ego with the Dream Team.

For those of you who may not have Spiritual Masters in your life, it is never too late to start. Their Love is available. I say why not accept it! We need all the help we can get, and Their Help is beyond mere thoughts and beliefs. Their Help borders on the Miraculous.

OVERCOMING TENSION

Tension is caused by negative thoughts. We can let go on any thought that causes the tension. One can discover the thought by merely saying this: "The negative thought causing this tension is_____."

Fill in the blank.

Let go of the thought, "I don't know." You do know. And you can access this thought and breathe it out.

When we choose peace and joy, anything causing tension goes out.

Peace and joy are more powerful than any negative thought, that is for sure. They can drown out the tension anytime. There is a lesson in ACIM that states this: "I choose the joy of God instead of pain." (ACIM; Lesson #190)

Beautiful lesson!

If we have a thought that something we are doing is "tedious", then we create tension. We should say that everything we do is an act of worship and not label it as tedious.

People think tension is normal. It is not.

Saying, "I am filled with God's love," dissolves tension.

One should consciously SEND LOVE to the area where there is a feeling of tension.

OVERCOMING WORRY

Worry is the opposite of faith. We must become conscious when we are worrying and stop it. If we could step back and let Him (the Christ) lead the way, there would be nothing to worry about. If we could say, "I place the future in the hands of God," (Lesson #194 in ACIM) there would be nothing to worry about.

Worry causes pain in the body.

The pandemic made us nervous. We have to learn to not get nervous about anything.

When we catch ourselves worrying, switch it to, I have faith that _____. Fill in the blank. Put anything positive in there. Anything but worry.

Worry is an attack on oneself.

When we catch ourselves worrying, switch it to, "I have faith that _____." Fill in the blank. Put anything positive there. Anything but worry.

Worry is an attack on oneself.

OVERCOMING SUFFERING

Suffering is a pattern. It can be an addiction. We may think we need to suffer to be Holy. This is false religious theology.

One has to say, "I give up my addiction to suffering to the Holy Spirit."

We have to forgive the church for teaching us suffering is Holy. We have had that programming for lifetimes. Are we ready to let go of church dogma and not feel guilty about doing that?

One can give up one's suffering to SHIVA. Shiva is the part of God that destroys ignorance. When we say we are giving it up to Shiva, we are saying that we really, really, don't want it anymore. We have to have a real conviction to give it up.

The addiction to suffering is one of the reasons prayers for healing do not work. We could have the exact right prayer; but if we are still addicted to suffering, then we will unconsciously keep the problem so we can suffer!

"God in His mercy wills that I be saved [from suffering]." (ACIM Lesson #235)

God does NOT want us to suffer. God's will for us is perfect happiness.

We tend to think about things that are bothering us instead of good things. It is an addiction to focus on what is bothering us. But that will only increase what is bothering us.

When we are sick and suffering, it means we lowered our frequency and then we became susceptible to bad things.

When one gets older, there is more of the past accumulated, and therefore, our life can get heavier and heavier. We experience less and less joy. The baby, who has no past (in this lifetime anyway) is therefore more joyous. The less past we cling to, the more joy we have now.

One should say this: "I trade in suffering for laughter and joy!"

To give up suffering we must master this thought: "I can be free of suffering today." (ACIM; Lesson #340)

For a long-term illness, we can write out ALL that happened from the beginning of the illness, all we tried to do to heal it, and all the feelings we had about the whole thing. Also, look at what was going on in our life just prior to having the illness, and forgive all of that. Get it all out on paper and then burn it and turn it over to the Holy Spirit entirely. Step back and let Him lead the way.

Empathy does not mean joining in the suffering of another. We must not lower ourselves to the level of the person's frequency who is in need of the healing. It is our job to lift them out of the cause of their suffering into a state of joy. And for this we must maintain our own connection to joy.

If we are suffering from a condition, it would be helpful to ask ourselves, "What are we punishing ourselves for by having this condition?"

We have to get in touch with the part of our mind that does not want things to work, the part of our mind addicted to suffering.

Empathy does not mean joining in the suffering of another. We must not lower ourselves to the level of the person's frequency who is in need of the healing. It is our job to lift them out of the cause of their suffering into a state of joy. And for this we must maintain our own connection to joy.

OVERCOMING GRIEF

When a loved one dies, it is not good to stuff one's feelings and avoid the grieving. Later that could become a long depression or mental ailment.

At the same time, it is important to see that we are Spiritual Beings. The soul of our loved one decides to go back to the non-physical state of being, and leave the body. There is no real "death" in this transition.

Usually, our grief is for ourself. We pity ourself for not having that person with us anymore. Perhaps we had a dependency on them for our sense of well-being. Perhaps we used them for a sense of our own emotional "security." Now they are gone and we are fearful and angry we are alone without them.

Or perhaps we have some guilt associated with them, and our past relationship with them. Their transition brings up this guilt in us. And we associate that guilt with our grief we are feeling.

Seeing our innocence and theirs would relieve our grief.

Seeing our independence and not our co-dependence would relieve our grief.

Seeing that they did not "die," but merely left a worn-out form, would relieve our grief.

LETTING GO

There is a very moving story. Tara Singh (Markus's teacher) asked Krishnamurti (who was Tara Singh's master) the following question:

"Does life take care?"

Krishnamurti answered:

"Yes, if you completely let go."

How does one let go completely? Start with the willingness. (Of course, one cannot be lazy.)

We are letting go when we allow God to take over. Consider this prayer:

I am one with Christ. Christ is taking over my whole life.

- ❖ *Christ is taking over my relationships.*
- ❖ *Christ is taking over all my affairs.*
- ❖ *Christ is taking over my whole body.*

Letting go completely is actually fun. But people don't tend to believe that. The ego tries to tell us that it is hard to do, or unpleasant, and we just cannot do it.

We have to be more interested in letting go totally than we are in any condition we have. We have to say that we are no longer interested in the

I am one with Christ. Christ is taking over my whole life.

- ❖ *Christ is taking over my relationships.*

- ❖ *Christ is taking over all my affairs.*

- ❖ *Christ is taking over my whole body.*

condition. We are not going to let it occupy our mind.

When we let go totally, it is not something shocking. It is just that we will suddenly feel really, really, good!

When someone withdraws from our life, we should simply just let go and say this: "Sending you tons of love." Why fret? Let go—someone better will come.

The reason it is so hard to let go of a person in our life is because we are attached to him or her. If you know someone better would replace them, would you hang on?

The reason it is so hard to let go of a condition in the body is because there is so much ego involved. The more complicated the disease, the stronger the ego. When you cut your finger, not so much ego is involved so it heals rapidly. For complicated diseases, there is more fear, anger and guilt involved.

When we let go, we feel good. If an incident happens that is unpleasant, we should not dwell on it. Let it go! Going over and over it in one's head puts one in a very low frequency.

How quickly can we let go of it? Liberation Breathing will help. Breathing in this way is totally a practice of letting go.

It is good if one can express one's feelings about the situation to someone. If no one is there, write a letter to God about it.

Once we *own our part* in creating the situation or incident, we can make amends and let it go. We should not let anything get us down. We should not worry about anything. We should not beat ourselves up about anything at all. Let it go!

Completing or letting go of a relationship should be a cause for celebration, not for guilt, regret, and punishment! One is completing a pattern when one ends a relationship. But one must learn not to repeat the pattern in the next relationship.

Some people beat themselves up in their next relationship because they "failed" in the last one. Maybe it was not a failure at all. Maybe it was a success to end a pattern. Let it go!

X is over. We should no longer need to re-visit this issue anymore.

Letting go of Church dogma: If we have left our religion and are on another spiritual path, fine. But it is recommended that one go back to the church where one was indoctrinated and forgive all that was false religious theology. Let it all go. Sit in the pew and forgive it all and let it all go. If it is needed to take communion on that day, fine. Whatever it takes. ACIM is a correction of religion.

When we have an emotional pattern that is not serving us, forgive it to let it go. Forgive oneself. We may have kept this pattern because we did not know how to replace it. But we can discover something better if we try.

Letting go all the way equals being totally relaxed. We must be willing to let go all the way and we don't have to know how to do it. The intention is what matters.

Letting go equals happiness.

One must be willing to let go of anything that is not the Atonement. The Atonement is complete forgiveness. The Atonement is the correction of all our wrong-thinking.

A lot of people wait until they are totally fed up before they will let go of a pattern. The minute you recognize the pattern the first time, let it go to the Holy Spirit.

We must be willing to LET GO of anything that is not our Real Self. What is not Pure Joy is not our Real Self.

ACHIEVING RELAXATION

It is okay to be totally relaxed. One would think one would not have to say this; but many people have relaxation associated with laziness and so they won't let themselves relax. Or they may think they don't even deserve to be relaxed.

One can be totally relaxed while doing work. In fact, that is a very important goal.

Some people think if they relax, something terrible will happen. Being uptight is normal for them and being relaxed is not normal. Make it normal to be relaxed.

God's Voice speaks to us all through the day and if we allow ourselves to hear it, we will feel good; therefore, we can be relaxed.

We can be relaxed in the Joy of God.

We need to be a lot more relaxed. We want to be happy *and relaxed.*

Happiness makes us relaxed. Relaxation makes us happy. They go together.

The pandemic made us nervous. Being nervous is fear.

The Presence of Babaji in our lives makes us more relaxed.

HAVING SAFETY

When we have certainty that God takes care of us, we will be safe.

"Your peace is with me Father, I am safe."

This is Lesson #245 in A Course in Miracles. It is a Lesson in Part II of the Workbook, and is very beautiful. It is poetic in its prayerful form.

Your peace surrounds me, Father. Where I go, Your peace goes there with me. It sheds its light on everyone I meet. I bring it to the desolate and lonely and afraid. I give Your peace to those who suffer pain, or grieve for loss, or think they are bereft of hope and happiness. Send them to me, my Father. Let me bring Your peace with me. For I would save Your Son, as is Your Will, that I may come to recognize my Self.

Our peace is to be shared, and in this sharing, we realize we have peace to give. When we have something true to give another, then we are protected, and we are safe.

All is well in the world of a person who has something of his or her own to give. Their joy increases as they give joy to others.

We can easily come to this inner sense of safety by simply asking ourselves, "What do I want to give?"

HEALING

We will be healed when we are ready to be healed.

Say this: "I am ready to let go of this condition. I have no more need for it."

We have to turn over the condition. Say this:

❖ *Holy Spirit, I no longer deny You Your ability to bestow Your Blessing of Healing onto me.*

❖ *I let go of my power trip of not letting anyone heal me so I could be the "king."*

Sickness is competition with God. Wanting to be "king" is wanting to keep the ego and overcome God.

One should try not to go down to the vibration of the condition. There are so many other wonderful things one can acknowledge to stay high and out of the vibration of sickness.

When we are experiencing a symptom in the body, we tend to start a battle with it. There is another way. Say this to your symptom: "I am grateful to this symptom for teaching me X."

Listen to hear what the "X" is. The symptom is trying to teach you something about yourself. Usually, it is a habitual pattern of thoughts or behaviors that needs to be corrected.

Guilt always blocks healing.

One must give up all anger at oneself in order to be healed.

There is a Hawaiian form of healing called Ho'Oponopono. It goes something like this:

As the Mother of my conscious mind, I talk to my Child of my subconscious mind. I ask my Child to join me in sending this problem up to the Father of my superconscious mind, which is the Holy Spirit.

The Holy Spirit sends our petition to solve our problem up to our Divine Creator, Who sends down the Mana (forgiveness) to dissolve this problem (which is an illusion).

The illusion made fear real. Our fear made the illusion real.

We must try to see this important thing:

All symptoms and diseases are an opportunity for us to process out the ego (which caused them in the first place), and therefore, become more enlightened.

Healing (whatever our problem or symptom happens to be) is a chance to get closer to God.

Christ healed people by not making the patient's symptoms or conditions real. He ONLY saw their perfection. He saw them clearly without their symptoms. He saw only our Real Self.

The Real Self is not sick. The Real Self is not even the body. The Real Self is Spirit which is in a state of grace forever.

One day our condition will just be over—finished—if we keep remembering not to make it real. We must not identify with the body and make the condition real. If we give it a label (like a diagnosis) that makes it more real, more solid.

The body itself is only a tool that we keep for service of communication. The body is only a communication device. The problem is we confuse our Identity with our body, and do not connect with our Higher Self. The body is just a vehicle to get us to our Inner Peace that we share, using the body to communicate to others that Inner Peace.

When we have a pain or discomfort in the body, one should rub the area while saying, "I put Jesus and Babaji and the Divine Mother right here." We can delegate them to heal us of any symptoms.

The more we choose to feel good, the faster we will be healed.

When we are NOT healed and have a continuing condition, it is hard to feel good. And yet, if we do things that make us feel good anyway, this helps the condition to be healed. In other words, we must insist to focus on things that make us feel good, even when we are in the middle of feeling bad.

Peace and joy and relaxation are ingredients for healing. Of course, we also need the right affirmations to correct the negative thoughts that caused the condition. Affirmations are miraculous healing thoughts. We decide to think these thoughts instead of the ones that caused our problems. Healing is a decision—just like sickness is a decision. We decide to think with positive, health-affirming thoughts.

One needs to have CERTAINTY that one can be totally healed.

One needs to stop thinking about the part of the body not doing well, and think about perfection instead.

When we have a symptom in our body, it is the body's way of trying to get rid of something in one's past. One has to find out what thing in the past one is hanging on to. One has to then turn that over to the Holy Spirit.

"The past is over. It can touch me not." This is Lesson #289 in ACIM.

Letting go of the past is easier than trying to wrestle with the symptom.

The condition is a "gift" to show us where we were stuck in the past, and what we need to forgive from our past, in order to be healed and free of the painful symptom.

All parts of the body are healed when we stay in the dimension of our perfection! This perfection is in the present, not the past. It is in peace, not inner conflict. Perfection is God's Healing Voice keeping all things in our life safe—and this includes the health of our mind and body.

We should say this: I now clear my mind of anything that would oppose my complete healing. I am ready for the Holy Spirit to heal me. I allow it. I allow my

We should say this:

I now clear my mind of anything that would oppose my complete healing. I am ready for the Holy Spirit to heal me. I allow it. I allow my body to reflect this healing of my mind. The Holy Spirit corrects all my errors in my mind with Truth.

body to reflect this healing of my mind. The Holy Spirit corrects all my errors in my mind with Truth.

If one has pain, one should put one's hands on the area and say:

"I allow Babaji to enter here. I allow Jesus to enter here. I allow the Divine Mother to enter here. And I put my perfection here."

One has to forgive oneself if the healing is taking a long time. If we judge ourselves for that, that judgement makes it even harder to heal the condition. One must love oneself and have gratitude to be alive instead.

Sometimes we speak the right words for healing, but the body has to catch up. There may be a delay.

One is ripping oneself off from joy by keeping a symptom.

One should put one's hands on the area that needs healing and say:

"I thank you for being my teacher; I bless you."

One has to be clear that one's desire to have one's prayers answered is stronger than the addiction to suffering.

How does one get over doubt and lack of faith when one has a long-term illness? One has to realize that the lack of faith and doubt were partly responsible for the condition. One has to learn how to STAY in certainty and faith all the time, and that will prevent illness. That is a state of consciousness one should and can achieve.

It seems hard to have faith when one's illness is roaring. But that is when one needs faith the most.

One should even give to the Holy Spirit the part of the body that is badly affected.

We have to be finished with the pattern that is behind the condition.

We need to talk to our condition like we would to a friend. Interview it!

We need to choose happiness over any payoff we are getting from the condition. What is a payoff? It is a neurotic benefit.

We must realize that we would rather feel God's joy in our body instead of pain and discomfort. We can let it go and let in God's joy.

One has to be willing to give up one's "obsession" with the ailment. One has to be willing to come to harmony with the condition and that makes one closer to giving it up.

One has to make peace with the symptoms and not be in a fight with them. One should try saying, "I see the good in you. You are my teacher."

We never create something in our body that we cannot uncreate.

Miracles enable you to heal the sick and raise the dead because you made sickness and death yourself, and can therefore abolish both. You are a miracle, capable of creating in the likeness of your Creator. (ACIM, TEXT, Chapter 1, Section i, ¶ 24)

Summary of Healing Prayers

- ❖ *I am the perfect love of God.*
- ❖ *Therefore, I am always perfect.*
- ❖ *I am always innocent.*
- ❖ *All guilt is gone.*
- ❖ *All fear is gone.*
- ❖ *All anger is gone.*
- ❖ *All resistance is gone.*
- ❖ *All unwillingness is gone.*
- ❖ *All rebellion is gone.*
- ❖ *Therefore, I have no more need for this condition now.*
- ❖ *All the symptoms are gone.*

One can also say, "I am ready to experience my perfection in the area of my body that had the problem."

Summary of Healing Prayers:

- ❖ I am the perfect love of God.
- ❖ Therefore, I am always perfect.
- ❖ I am always innocent.
- ❖ All guilt is gone.
- ❖ All fear is gone.
- ❖ All anger is gone.
- ❖ All resistance is gone.
- ❖ All unwillingness is gone.
- ❖ All rebellion is gone.
- ❖ Therefore, I have no more need for this condition now.
- ❖ All the symptoms are gone.

The Love of God will heal us but we have to let it in. One has to be willing to let in God's perfect love, God's perfect peace, and God's perfect Joy to replace the negative mental mass that caused the symptom.

For lengthy illnesses or conditions, one tends to get the thought, "I might never get over this." That thought stops the healing! Confess it to the Holy Spirit.

The illness takes us down to the bottom of our ego and we should be grateful that the illness is pointing out the ego.

A "miracle healing" is not scary. It is merely the body going back to normal.

Speak to the affected area. Say this:
"I am so grateful to my (area in need of healing). It has served me so well. Thank you." I know someone who healed

himself of lung cancer by doing only this twice a day in front of his altar.

Getting really excited over something will promote healing.

One must turn over the whole condition and outcome to the Holy Spirit.

We have to love it to heal it. We must love the part of our body that hurts.

Ingredients for healing: Love of oneself and gratitude.

Accepting Joy will heal us. Joy is available. Express it now.

Peace itself is very healing. Claim it.

Praising others will help heal them, and you as well. Praise them.

Showing gratitude will heal you. Thanking the part of your body that is sick will heal it.

And here is the biggie:

"The cause of all sickness is ALWAYS the wish to die and overcome Christ."

Everyone has to face this for himself.

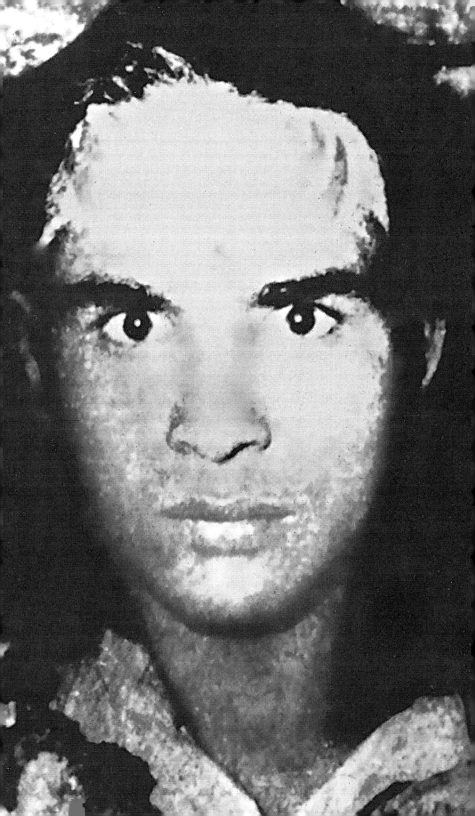

GOD

When we have created the hugest painful dramas that just don't go away, we tend to think that God is not there for us. But it is because we had that thought (that God is not there for us) long ago, that we attract the dramas.

It is the ultimate trick of the ego to tell us that God is not there for us, that God is letting us down, not giving us the help we want. God is always there to help us, but because we imagined we separated from Him, we think He is not there. That thought we have had for eons. It is like saying there is no God.

All negative dramas and illnesses are competition with God. Why is it that we are competition with God? The ego is trying to prove that God is dead and not here for us.

One can remove major chunks of drama if one gets that it is never true that God is not here for us.

Often, we are holding onto an illness because we are afraid that if we let it go, we would get close to God. The ego cannot stand that.

All negative dramas and illnesses are competition with God. Why is it that we are in competition with God? The ego is trying to prove that God is dead and not here for us.

One can remove major chunks of drama if one gets that it is never true that God is not here for us.

WRITING
THE MASTER

When we do confess something to a Master, it does release our guilt.

One can write to his or her Master. Confessing something to one's guru in a letter is so much better than going to someone else. The guru will not lay any guilt onto us. We will feel much better to release the issue, than keep it inside of us.

Write a responsible letter like this:

Dear Babaji,

1) This is my problem (only write about one problem at a time).
2) These are my thoughts that made up this problem (take 100% responsibility and confess them).
3) I am sorry for these thoughts.
4) These are my new thoughts (write the opposite of each thought in 2)
5) Please add Your Energy to my new thoughts.
6) Thank You. I am grateful for Your help.

Sign your name and date it.

Put the letter under the Altar Cloth on your Altar and expects a shift.

ADVANCING

We are supposed to ADVANCE. But we usually feel unsafe going to the next level. We need to get that it is actually more fun, easier and safer. That is because as we advance, we are getting closer to God. God is the only safety there is.

Babaji once told me, "Advance!"

GETTING STRONGER

We should keep saying that we are getting stronger every year. Every day, in fact.

This is a very important affirmation because people think that they get weaker as they get past 60. We can live as long as we chose while improving our bodies. (See our book on Physical Immortality: bit.ly/ImmortalRay)

One should be able to feel as good at 80 as one felt at 20. The energy for that is still here in the universe. It is still within us.

FUTURE

It is good to keep thinking "Everything will be alright." People usually have the subconscious thought that things won't work out in the future, or that something bad will happen. When something bad happens, we start worrying that something else bad will happen.

Say this: "I place the next moment in the hands of God."

What if we took the affirmation, "Only good things happen to me." We might not believe that at first; but if we keep saying it, that is the result we will get.

Most people in old age aren't having any fun because they are thinking about the fact that they are closer to death.

There *is another way.*

We write here about an alternative to death—*Physical immortality: How to Overcome Death.*

Can we have fun as an elder even if we don't have grandchildren?

Yes, if we are getting deeper on the spiritual path.

One has to be willing to go to the next level, even if unknown.

One could say, "I am going to make the next 20 or 30 years to be FUN."
Gratitude replaces complaining. One must do this.

When you have total gratitude for everything (every little thing), the universe will be so glad to take care of you!!

PERFECTION

Some people have a fear of perfection, because in church we were told it is blasphemous to think we are perfect. And yet, in the Bible it says, "Be ye therefore perfect, even as your Father which is in heaven is perfect." (Matthew 5:48)

That is a huge contradiction and gets us all confused.

If we are expressing our perfection, then there would never be anything to worry about. God's will for us is to manifest our divine perfection.

When we allow perfection, we will be free of fear and we can and will hear God and feel really good. We will also be able to repair symptoms quickly.

If we accept our perfection, we can create perfectly with our thoughts and get our bodies to be perfect (with no symptoms).

Anything contradicting our perfection, we can lovingly let it go.

We should say this: I am in the dimension of my perfection. I am also in the dimension of God's perfection because I am one with God.

We should remain aware that we are in the dimension of our perfection. This changes everything.

We should say this: I am in the dimension of my perfection. I am also in the dimension of God's perfection, because I am one with God.

We should remain aware that we are in the dimension of our perfection. This changes everything.

If we decide to *stay* in the dimension of our perfection, there is nothing that can cause trouble.

The dimension of our perfection is bliss. We can allow ourselves to feel that right now. It is safe. It is only more of good feelings. Imagine walking around feeling good all the time.

We *are* God's perfect love. This is really a high thought and solves everything. If we got that, then our problems would disappear.

God's perfect love created us in perfect love so we are perfect. God does not add any imperfection in there. But we do. We put things in us that are not who we are.

We must choose God's perfect love as our Identity. If we simply recognize that we are God's perfect love, lower-level things will disappear.

We must allow God's perfect love to take over our whole life! This is our true frequency.

We must live in our true frequency.

Pain is the part of our mind that has not accepted that we are perfect love, or the part of our mind that has not chosen joy.

Since God sees me perfect, why shouldn't I?

It is good to say this:

I am perfect love.
I am perfect innocence.
I am perfect peace.

FEELING GOOD

When we allow the perfection of God to move through our life, that means we will always be feeling good.

Feeling good should be our top priority.

Observing one's thoughts and raising the quality of each thought continuous-ly makes one feel good.

When we have a grateful thought, we cannot have an anxious thought.

When we are having a thankful thought, we cannot have a worry thought.

Doing a spiritual practice makes one feel good.

It feels good to move forward.

We should train ourselves to have exalted thoughts so we can feel good.

What is the secret of feeling good? Answer: Letting go of our "case" and giving our attention to joy.

One can feel better by writing out one's feelings and especially by writing a letter to the Dream Team (Jesus, Babaji & Divine Mother).

You may have your own Spiritual Master in whom you implicitly trust.

We should align with the thoughts of a Spiritual Master, like Jesus, Babaji or the

Divine Mother. Then we can THINK LIKE GOD. We will then definitely feel good.

We could have the affirmation: "I no longer make up problems."

Say this: "I am willing to feel good all over my body." Say: "I am feeling really good doing what I am doing right now."

We have been addicted to feeling bad. "Heaven is a decision we must make." (Lesson #138 in ACIM)

Say this: "My whole day is the Divine moving through me."

The more we choose to feel good, the faster we will be healed.
Say, "I let go into the flow of feeling good. I flow in that direction."

To feel good, celebrate when you complete something. (Even if it is the end of a relationship!)

The Dream Team will help us to feel good.

We must keep thinking this: "Everything is going to be alright," and
"Only good things happen to me from now on."

Anything unlike the joy of God can now lovingly be released.

Staying in the dimension of our perfection equals not only feeling good, it is actually bliss!

Letting go makes us feel good. Doing only what we want to do makes us feel good.

Deep circular breathing makes us feel really good.

Staying in present time makes us feel good.

Meditating on the Divine Mantra makes us feel good.

Making our space impeccable feels good.

We should write down what makes us feel good.

Knowing that our work is worship makes us feel good.

Service makes us feel good.
Keeping a gratitude journal makes us feel good.

Practicing the principle of right association feels good. (Hanging around those people in a higher dimension.)

Giving compliments that are real makes us feel good.

Laughter yoga feels good.

Every day we are feeling better than the day before.

Getting closer to God makes us feel better.

Most people settle for feeling bad or for feeling just okay. We should always be feeling better than that. We could feel bliss. "Heaven is the decision we must make." Remember this one line!

"I choose the joy of God instead of pain." (ACIM; Lesson #190) This is statement that makes us feel good.

We should help people change their life from a bad dream to a happy dream.

We must want to know what it is like to feel as good as possible.

If we would choose to be our Real Self, we would feel good all the time.

We should get grounded in the ACIM Lesson, "I am as God created me." That way bad energy cannot enter.

Giving up fear is what makes us feel good.

People put up with feeling okay or feeling fine—but what about feeling REALLY GOOD? Go for THAT!

Many people have a fear of feeling too good. They think something terrible will happen. And yet, feeling good attracts more of feeling good if we change that thought.

We have to be willing to FEEL God's Love in order to feel good.

"I feel the Love of God within me now." (ACIM; Lesson #189)

We must train ourself to feel good no matter what is happening.

Enjoyment equals self-love, which equals more enjoyment. Think about having "sheer enjoyment."

Enjoyment equals self-love, which equals more enjoyment. Think about having "sheer enjoyment."

HAVING FUN

Expressing the opposite of our personal lie is fun.

It is fun to be alive. The more we get enlightened, the more alive we are and the more alive we are, the more fun we have.

When we are at a big moment in transformation, it does not have to be scary. It can be fun!

When we let go of fear of being closer to our Guru, we will have more fun.

Without anger, our fun is unlimited.

We could decide that for the next 20-30 years we are going to have more fun daily.

Then after 30 years, see where we are.

SEX

If people have a sexual problem, it is probably due to shame and guilt.

We should consciously invite God into our lovemaking, moment by moment. Most people are hesitant to do this because they don't have God and sex wired together in their minds, and that is the problem.

Sex is like anything else in life. Are we turning it over to the sacred? Everything about sex is sacred, but we forget to bring it into the highest vibration of holiness.

This is a moment-to-moment thing. I like what the Kahunas in Hawaii say, "Every atom of creation is alive and therefore sacred." They consider the Divine Forces of Life permeate everything—even the smallest particle of dust.

When we make sex sacred, it can only bring us joy. It is an honoring of our partner in the intercourse of joy.

Giving is the key to great sex. What do we have to give our partner in the form of Love in the sexual play of energy?

When we give to another, this is very arousing.

Especially when that person is someone with whom we have entrusted the mutual care for our soul.

We care for the soul of our lover, and they care for ours.

This exchange is a lifting up of energies of the sexual body, through the mental body, to the ultimate spiritual body that melds with our Creator.

The Divine Father of spiritual connection melds with the Divine Mother of corporeal manifestation and ignites in a Union of Sacred Fire.

This Fire of Sexual Bond is the crucible out of which all Life springs forth.

Even if this is a Child of Blissful experience, we are only filled with Joy.

We forget ourselves in this sacred joining. Two become One.

Sex is Innocence.

Sex is Fun.

Sex is Sacred.

Sex is Enlightening.

Sex is a Spiritual Practice.

Sex is an Expander of Consciousness.

Sex is what we put into it in terms of our intention.

It can be totally profane. It can be totally sacred. The choice is ours in our approach and in our intention.

LOVE

The love between oneself and God, or oneself and the Guru, needs to keep growing.

Self-love is key. It may feel weird to out-and-out love oneself, but try it and keep trying it until you feel it.

One way to love oneself is to say, "I am so grateful to be alive." Saying this feels good and feeling good is always a way to love oneself.

RELATIONSHIPS

We must relate to each other as God. If I relate to someone as God, then they are perfect.

The more the merrier. The more people the merrier. The more students the merrier. The more clients the merrier. The more friends the merrier.

Regarding our relationship with God, we must be able to have a regular conversation with God.

We can use the mantra for healing our relationship when it gets stuck. Lie down together and breathe to it together, holding hands.

Instead of disapproving of your mate for something you don't like, say this: "What I would really like is if you could do it this way: _____."

Give them the inspirational thought that will make them want to change. We can also state what we need and want from them.

Example: "What I want is for you to speak to me in a calm and gentle tone." Example: "What I want is that you give very careful attention when it comes to financial matters."

When one's mate is going through something heavy, one can also talk about how they are not alone because we have something going on also.

When we don't like something our mate is doing, we can bring it up; but we must remember to be really NICE about it. Criticism kills relationships.

Two minutes of an upset is too much. One minute is too much. One has to imagine no upsets.

Early on in the relationship, one should tell one's mate what things are "up" to be worked on in oneself, and ask the mate to help release that. Both should do this.

In a holy relationship two people come together for the evolution of their souls.

Each partner helps the other ascend. Therefore, they become "Ascension Buddies."

REASONS PEOPLE "SETTLE FOR LESS" IN A RELATIONSHIP

1. Low self-esteem
2. Not even asking for what one wants from the universe
3. Addiction to one's personal lie
4. Punishment for unconscious guilt
5. Fear of asking partner to "show up" and be great
6. Copying parents' relationship
7. Thinking it is not okay to leave
8. Fear if one leaves, one would end up alone
9. Being addicted to suffering
10. Letting the ego rule instead of the Holy Spirit
11. Fear of being really alive and in one's power

12. Staying in one's comfort zone (addicted to what is familiar even if it feels really bad)
13. Getting some neurotic "payoff"
14. Thinking it is not possible to have a great relationship
15. Struggle pattern
16. Past life karma
17. Fear of total aliveness and joy
18. Wanting to stay angry
19. Not having any idea how to create enlightenment
20. Ignorance of creative thought
21. Loving to complain
22. Not forgiving parents and past relationships
23. Addiction to conflict
24. Fear of change
25. Spiritual laziness

Are you stuck in one of these? We have to give them all up!

RECIPE FOR A GREAT RELATIONSHIP

1. Remove all negativity.

2. Treat your mate like you would an honored guest.

3. Choose to forgive your mate, and whatever is happening with you and your mate, on the spot.

4. When you are angry, be determined NOT TO SPEAK. After you calm down you should say this to your mate: "I know I was feeling activated and I am sorry. The negative thought that I had that made me

feel activated was _____." It is then good to have a Liberation Breathing session to breathe out any remaining anger.

5. Remember that criticism kills relationships. Use the 8-minute process for communicating tough issues.

6. Instead of using anger, always say instead: "I am feeling activated. The negative thought that is making me activated right now is_____."
(suggested by Babaji)

7. To solve ALL conflicts, ALWAYS play the Highest Spiritual Thought Game.

8. See your mate as your guru. You NEVER would attack your guru.

9. Do daily devotions together every morning.
10. Make A Course in Miracles and

Liberation Breathing your spiritual path. Get sessions from a well-trained Breathworker frequently.

11. Link up with the Dream Team and make an altar to them: (Babaji; Jesus of ACIM; and the Divine Mother—Amma).

12. Take the Loving Relationships Training (The LRT®) together as a couple, and review it as often as necessary to master it.

13. Read these books: I Deserve Love/ Loving Relationships/ Spiritual Intimacy.

bit.ly/DeserveRay
bit.ly/NLRBRay
bit.ly/SpiritualRay

PROSPERITY

God will always prosper us; but we have to be willing to receive. And we have to clear out our family dynamic on money.

Many people get stuck at the same financial ceiling as their parents. That is not necessary.

We have to turn over that pattern to the Holy Spirit and raise our self-esteem to receive more money.

"God is raining financial blessings on our business."

"*God is raining financial blessings on our business.*"

We only take on projects that we are certain will succeed.

One can take on more projects and still have it easy.

We all want to experience abundance and be safe with it. That is totally possible.

The Divine Mother wants us to have everything we desire, easily. The key is gratitude for what we already have, which is everything already.

PRAYER

Everyone should have a prayer room or at least a "prayer corner."

Spending a lot of time there praying will help us greatly, to get to the point that nothing bothers us.

One should pray to be attentive to one's Christ Self. We can actually ask, "Christ, please teach me to ascend."

One must want to become what Christ wants us to become.

Our "Christ Self" is merely our true, God-created nature.

If we turn over something to the Holy Spirit to change, or we go away and it does not happen, that means something in our subconscious is blocking that process.

Ask to be shown your block and be willing to say to the "block," "I'm sorry; Please forgive me; I love you; Thank you."

We have to have a love for self-correction.

God's will for us is perfect happiness. So, if we are not feeling the happiness, we obviously have something to correct.

Correction is easy for the Holy Spirit. In fact, it is effortless.

When we admit we are "wrong," and we are if we are not happy, then Divine Forces can restore us to peace and joy.

We don't have to "fix things." We simply have to let go.

Inner correction is a way of life.

More and more joy is a result of surrendering "problems" over to the Great Unknown for solution.

Divine Forces and the Great Unknown are the same.

The Unknown is benevolent to our needs. God provides for our needs before we even need them.
Prayer is opening our channel to give and receive from God.

Prayer is the end of separation.

Prayer blesses everyone.

Prayer forgives everyone.

Prayer includes everyone.

Prayer uplifts everyone.

Prayer is constant.

Prayer is attentive.

Prayer receives.

Prayer gives.

Prayer Loves.

JOY

We must let go of everything in opposition to peace and joy. We don't even have to know all that is in us in opposition to peace and joy. But to be willing to give it up is the important thing.

Say this: Anything unlike the joy of God can now be lovingly released in me.

We should not use our body as a scapegoat to sabotage our joy. (We do that by making up symptoms and projecting them onto the body.)

We would like to have ONLY JOY! Then we have to have all of our thoughts be only joyful. (This is a real spiritual discipline; we should try and see if we can do that.)

If we have only joyful thoughts, how could the body have pain? The joy in us is taking over the whole body!

The thought on ONLY JOY will take out the tension in our bodies.

The joy in one's heart takes over the tension and releases it.

We can say this: "I am having joy doing this_____!"

We can say "I am filled with joy and I feel it!"

We need to find out what makes us joyful and do more of that.

We need to give thanks when we are joyful and then the joy will increase.

The joy is always here because God is always here. But sometimes we cover it up.

One day soon we will have certainty that we are always in joy. People tend to have the thought that joy won't last.

We thought we had to do something to get joy—but it is really that we have to REMOVE something to feel the joy that is always there. What are we covering it up with?

If we allow ourselves to feel the Master's love, we will be in joy and bliss.

Sometimes we cannot have joy when completing things because there might be a death in the family for example. And yet to overcome the grief, it is good to do things that bring us joy. Once, after a death in my family, my teacher told me to go to a conservatory in an arboretum, and sit among the ferns and breathe in the life urge. It worked.

We CAN let anything go that is not joy. We CAN let go of anything that does not feel good. It is a decision.

It is a joy to feel good. We need to let perfection and joy take over our whole life.

Try saying, "I am in the Vibration of Babaji." Or, "I am in the vibration of Jesus." Or, "I am in the Vibration of the Divine Mother." This will bring joy. Or, "I am in the vibration of the Dream Team (all three)."

Our true Self is our God Self. We must learn to be constantly aware of our true Self to stay in joy.

It is possible to feel good all the times and stay in joy.

Say this, "I am receiving Divine energy right now and it feels so good."

Or say this, "I am receiving God's love."

That will bring joy.

"I can handle the joy."

Saying, "I AM the joy of God," will keep us from slipping back into problems.

We can do anything with our holiness that produces joy.

We should ENJOY everything we are doing! Every little thing.

We can say that we are letting go of anything that is not joy. The more I enjoy myself, the more the tension goes out.

We must keep trying to make our thoughts joyful.

One should be happy to trade in a negative pattern for joy.

We must weed out of our consciousness anything that does not lead to joy.

People like paying people who have joy. We can replace all tension with joy.

When we are feeling joy, we can expand it by doing a Liberation Breathing session. We should not just get rebirthed when one feels bad.

We can stay in joy as long as we do not add anything negative to our mind.

We should take time to enjoy the joy, not run away from it.

We have gone so far away from joy that we forgot how it felt, and we made up a fear about it.

Affirm, "I allow myself to feel the joy that is already in me. I am immediately relaxed into the joy."

Joy is contagious.

Say this, "I can feel the joy going up my spine."

Total joy and total success go together!

Can we honestly say, "I enjoy being here. I enjoy being alive all the time."

We need to say, "God's joy is healing me."

We get joy directly from the Divine Mother. She is supreme Joy.

Saying, "I am the Christ," will wipe out disturbances and lead to joy.

It is kind of a *sin* to be unhappy.

We should be able to say, "My whole life is pure joy!

We need to say,
"God's joy is healing
me."

We get joy directly
from the Divine
Mother. She is
supreme Joy.

Saying, "I am the
Christ," will wipe
out disturbances
and lead to joy.

CLARITY

When we are clear we can accomplish so much more!

Clarity comes when there is no guilt / no fear / no anger.

When we are clear, we can get really high.

Fun and joy merge when we give up fear, guilt, and anger.

When we are clear, we are totally relaxed automatically.

We should have the supreme intention to become clear.

We cannot try to manifest something while at the same time we have a fear that it won't work and we won't get it. That cancels out the result.

We must trade in anger for peace; guilt for innocence; fear for love; and sadness for joy. It can be done.

PHYSICAL IMMORTALITY

The death urge is unconscious. It takes courage to look at it and breathe it out. People think they will die if they feel their death urge so they don't even look at it. But the other option is keeping it which will surely cause death. It is better to face it and to go through temporary fear in a breathing session.

We have to give up all unconscious fears to keep from dying.

The guru will push up these fears in a way that is tolerable so they can be released.

After we have gone through tons of trials in our life and passed them, why would we not want to stick around and enjoy the benefits of all that? Give up aging!

We are actually etheric substance.

If we can get through the fear of death, we 'have it made."

The most important thing to say is: "I AM the resurrection and the life."

Spirit is that which cannot be destroyed. "I am Spirit, therefore I cannot be destroyed."

Mind is condensed Spirit, and Body is condensed Mind. Therefore, Body is utmost Spirit.

In this way, Body is transmuted to Spirit. It is then a communication device of immortality.

Physical Immortality is the ultimate unification of all dimensions of existence to transcend all differences.

Spirit—Mind—Body—Immortality.

ATONEMENT

We must accept the Atonement for ourselves and mean it. This means that we accept correction for all our wrong thinking and we accept total forgiveness. It also means we accept our Oneness with God.

We must start by accepting the Atonement for ourselves.

We must be willing to claim our perfection. We must be willing to claim our innocence. We need to say, "This will give us a bright future."

We must be willing to claim our perfection.

We must be willing to claim our innocence.

We need to say, "This will give us a bright future."

FAITH

Faith is unquestioning belief that does not require proof or evidence.

Nothing will be impossible with God. Had we not lacked faith that this thing could be solved, the problem would be gone!

There is no problem in any situation that faith would not solve.

Certainty is like having total faith.

Babaji says that, "Faith is Everything."

We cannot be healed without the faith that it is possible.

Remember the Bible verse, "In God, all things are possible."

Trust and faith lead to becoming like a jewel.

Have faith in this one thing: "God wills that we be in Heaven on earth."

There is not room enough in our mind for both worry and faith. We must decide which one gets to live there. Worry is the opposite of faith.

If we are saying we believe in God and yet we only have 80% faith, that 20% is saying God is not whole. That is insane.

We need to have total, 100% faith for it to be real.

Have faith
in this one
thing:
"God
wills that we
be in
Heaven
on earth."

We could say, "I will give up this fear when I get more faith," and, "I will get more faith when I give up this fear." Going round and round that way. Giving up fear seems impossible since it is an addiction.

We should read ACIM until we get fear is not even real.

We have to totally reclaim our faith all the way.

When we have total faith, we will be totally relaxed.

Faith is trusting in something we cannot prove. It is having an unshakable confidence.

There is often a subconscious thought that things will not work out. This is lack of faith.

Worry is the opposite of faith. Fear is the opposite of faith. Worry does not make us feel good.

We are dishonoring God by doubting. Faith gives glory to God. We can ask God to restore our faith where it was lost.

We need to say that faith is a gift we give ourselves.

The prescription we need is more faith. What percentage of faith do we have? 60%? Well, then the 40% lacking is like saying NO to the healing or change we want. Doubt is like saying NO.

Something new can always happen.

Put faith and love into the part of the body suffering.

If we say, "Everything is going to turn out well," and we say it enough, that will strengthen faith.

Where we have the least trust (say when things are going badly), that is exactly where we need to place the most faith.

We need to ask the Holy Spirit to strengthen our faith. We can ask the Holy Spirit to transfer to us the faith we need.

Fear closes out faith from coming in. Fear also forces out faith that was there. Fear makes us lose faith.

Saying that we have only 50% faith is like saying something is 50% wrong with God.

We need to say this, "Holy Spirit, please take away my doubt."

While we are waiting to be healed, praying and waiting, we must not get discouraged. We must keep doing the "right thing." (The right thing would be faith.)

The ego does not like faith. It will try to stop one's faith. When one really goes for total faith, there will be a "response column," perhaps. By that I mean anything unlike faith will come up. Fear for example.

When things are not working out, that is when we need more faith. But that is exactly when our faith is weak. This is tricky. How do we have more faith when things look bad? Pray for one's faith to be restored where it was lost.

Doubting really is dishonoring God. It's like saying God is not capable of creating the universe, or especially things in my universe. I think you can see how ridiculous this sounds.

When we lose all or some of our faith, then disasters can come.

When we let go of fear, faith rushes in. Faith is the opposite of fear.

Getting one's faith back is like getting one's "mojo" back! Faith gives us strength.

"Nothing will be impossible with God." Luke 1:37

There is no problem in any situation that faith would not solve.

An attitude of faith allows God to do amazing things! God has plenty of faith to share with us. And with faith God is able to "move mountains."

There is nothing more powerful than faith. It activates God's power.

Faith heals. And Faith prevents illness. That is important. Therefore, one must keep faith at all times, no matter what!

Faith is everything. Faith is the answer to every problem.

Having faith makes us a lot more clear.

When we have total faith, we will be totally relaxed.

There is faith, and then there is STAYING IN FAITH all the time completely.

Our faith and gratitude must be continuous, especially when things go wrong. That requires vigilance.

An attitude of faith allows God to do amazing things. Faith gives glory to God.

Praising God strengthens faith.

We need faith also in ourselves. What is our level of faith in ourselves, percentage wise????

Lending our faith to others who need it strengthens our own.

TRUTH

The truth liberates people. Sometimes people don't like the truth told to them. It is too much of a confrontation. But if we have the love of correction (which is very important), we WANT the truth.

Reading this book will be the antidote to the Kranti. Truth is the antidote for the Kranti. The Kranti is the period of global revolution Babaji predicted would happen, in which the old ways would break down and fall away.

WHO WE ARE

We think we have to do a lot to be all that we can be. And yet, God created us complete with the total blueprint. Therefore, we don't have to strive and work our butt off. If we accept the Atonement for ourselves, we are all that we are—already. There is nothing to *become*. We are already the perfect love of God.

What if our whole day is the Divine moving through us? This a very beautiful thought. If we allow the Divine to move through us, imagine how wonderful that would be? It would be joy.

The Divine Bliss. Actually, the Divine *is already* moving through us; but we are blocking it and not allowing it fully into our awareness. Who wouldn't want to be unblocked and *feel the Divine* moving through us? Why wouldn't we want this? Only if we think we don't deserve it.

We always want more of our Real Self. Every time we go the extra mile for someone, we get more of our Real Self. The only way out of big problems is for us to be our Real Self.

Saying, "I am the Christ," would be the truth. The truth will set us free.

Christ is teaching us to ascend.

We want to be able to experience our Real Self. This lesson is imperative, "I am as God created me." One should meditate on that one thought for many months.

We must only allow our Real Self to inhabit our mind / body.

There is nothing but total benefit by being our Real Self. When breathing we can say, "I let go of anything that is not my Real Self."

Fear, anger and guilt have no place in our Real Self. We let them go into the dust out of which they came.

They are illusions brought to the Truth to be dissolved.

The Christ in us will dissolve them, easily, if we allow this miracle to happen.

THE HOLY SPIRIT

The Holy Spirit is the big "gift giver." This Life Force will take away bad things from us, which would be a definite gift, AND will give us what we ask for.

One can say to the Holy Spirit, "I give up all my negative thoughts in my subconscious that I don't even know I have."

Say this, "All my negativity is dissolving with the Holy Spirit."

What does it mean when we say, "I am turning this over to the Holy Spirit?" We stop doing what we thought we had to do, and admit there is a new possibility that God will give to us that we have not seen or thought of before.

This new possibility is far better than the ones we thought of before.

THE DREAM TEAM

The *Dream Team* consists of Babaji, Jesus of ACIM, and the Divine Mother. With these three one has everything.

The Dream Team says we are precious stars and we should breathe in their love. We have to want to commune with the Dream Team.

We must give the Dream Team permission to direct us totally. It is FUN! The Dream Team can give us more fun than we can imagine. However, people don't usually associate fun with the Spiritual Masters.

Why go down when you can go up? We must stay at the level of the Dream Team. Not only can we relate to the Dream Team, we can join them and be ON the Dream Team.

We have not even begun to let in the real love of the Masters—maybe a little. But they have so much more to give us! We have to be open to receive God's love through the Dream Team and other channels.

When we give all of our mistakes to the Dream Team, we should say, "I give you all my mistakes of the past and even those of the present."

Are we riding on the energy of the Dream Team or not?

It is FUN talking to the Dream Team—like a sport....

We can FEEL the pleasure of the Divine Mother.

We now have Babaji's energy!! And Jesus guides our steps.

We are one with the Dream Team.

If something goes terribly OFF, we need to acknowledge in that moment the presence of the Dream Team.

If we can LET IN the Dream Team all the time, we would always feel magnificent.

We have to say we want to FEEL the love of the Dream Team.

If we are willing to MERGE with the Guru, then things would be cleared up totally. Total merging = ultimate gift to oneself.

SPIRITUAL PRACTICE

When one has been doing spiritual practices regularly, it is good to notice that one is therefore having more fun in life. When spiritual practices are done daily, most people do not associate that with fun. But the RESULT will be more fun in one's life. One can even learn to have fun doing the practices.

FASTING

If one fasts during Navaratri (Divine Mother Festival), one has more time to think about God and therefore, one feels better. Most people just think about food. They think about breakfast, eat breakfast; then think about lunch, eat lunch; then think about dinner, and eat dinner.

Giving your body a rest from digestion gives it a chance to reboot itself. Emptiness is next to Godliness.

Giving your body a rest from digestion gives it a chance to reboot itself. Emptiness is next to Godliness.

GRATITUDE

People should say out loud what they are grateful for, besides keeping a gratitude journal.

One does not need to say much more about gratitude here, because the topic has been covered thoroughly in the book *THE MAGIC*. Even if one thinks one knows all about this subject, one should still read it.

Out of immense gratitude, one is willing to do higher and higher levels of divine service. What does one do to sing praises at least once daily?

SURRENDER

We must finally choose to surrender totally, let go totally, and let the Divine take over our whole life.

We are afraid that if we give up control, something bad will happen. But, it is the other way around. Staying in control leads to bad things happening.

One has to want to give up control. We are afraid of it because we think if God controls us, God will make us do something we don't want to do! God only wants what brings us perfect happiness.

Giving up control is the end of the ego's rule. That is also salvation.

We have to want that bad enough that it overcomes the subconscious mind, which is a sabotage machine.

One has to say, "Above all else, I want to let go totally and surrender."

When we say, "I want the Holy Spirit to take over my whole life," that has to be a big act of faith also.

One should not "try hard" to surrender. It is just a question of letting go of any resistance to that surrender.

When one surrenders, the ego can no longer take over the mind. We are free.

There is no more fear.

One has decided for Heaven and will get that.

Then, God takes over.

- ❖ Only good things happen.
- ❖ One goes into one's greatness.
- ❖ One is safer.
- ❖ One is free of flaws.
- ❖ One gets "higher," i.e. more advanced.
- ❖ One gets rejuvenated.
- ❖ One can even become prettier and more handsome at any age.
- ❖ One gets constant happiness.
- ❖ One gets healed.
- ❖ One is closer to the Divine Mother Who is Opulent, so one becomes more opulent.
- ❖ One will be totally relaxed.

This is my Prayer of Surrender:

The Lord has healed me! My celebration is now eternal. I am free!

My guru took away my pain.

I praise His name forever. Shiva Om!

Joy is finally here!

I am the mantra and the mantra is me.

My gut was crying out—didn't know what to do.

My guru heard my prayers and answered me.

My ego has no chance in the Presence of His love.

Today I volunteer to tell the world of His Grace!

My True Self has emerged.

It was gone so long.

I am done with that pattern that enslaved me so long.

I feel His Bliss creeping in.

Oh, why was I gone so long from the truth?

I give Him that little part I left hanging on.

I see a new life ahead!

I can't stop my love from pouring out.

It is increasing day by day with His Grace.

Ambe Ma. Jagadambe Ma!

My heart is cracking,

To let my guru in even more.

How would I even know about the blessings of the Divine Mother,

Had my guru not led me to Her?

Oh, that I become a fountain of gratitude!

MIRACLES

Our body can now handle exciting miracles. If we totally let go of fear, we get miracles.

PART II

THE DIVINE MOTHER

THE DIVINE MOTHER

When I was doing my breathing meditations, I was mostly in touch with Babaji. But at some point, it was clear the Divine Mother wanted Her presence made known. She is the one Who gave us Liberation Breathing®. It is the Divine Mother's Gift to humanity.

Markus and I have dedicated our lives to bringing this healing modality to the people. It is our joy to do so.

A new action She wants us to share is Mantra Breathing. When we combine

Liberation Breathing with the reciting of a very High Thought—the mantra—the power of the process is increased exponentially.

In this Part II of *Outside the Box with Babaji*, He wants me to emphasize the importance of the Divine Mother in our spiritual lives.
The Divine Mother will help you achieve miracle consciousness.

You are entitled to miracles. I am very, very happy to be a messenger for the Divine Mother for you.

The original spark of creation is a feminine aspect. So here we are talking about the very primal force itself (the Source).

Some call Her the supreme Deity, the source of all knowledge, that which is beyond everything! Some describe Her as the intelligence behind matter. That is why in India they say that there is nothing higher than the Divine Mother. The great Saint Sri Aurobindo said that surrender to the Divine Mother is the final stage of perfection. It took me a long time to figure out that the "secret" of the saints and masters I met was just that:

Surrender to and worship of the Divine Mother.

It is said that the Divine Mother releases us from delusion. This is of maximum importance on the spiritual path. To make rapid spiritual progress, one must reach for the "deep", called the MA (the internal) rather than the Maya (the external). The sooner we all do this, the better for ourselves and the whole planet. The more we surrender to the Divine Mother, the faster will be our progress.

She will bring us to the nurturing, tender aspect of ourself, which is so needed to solve the huge problems we have today. The Divine Mother will bring all of us the solutions to our personal problems, as well as to our planetary problems. We need to let Her teach us now. By connecting to Her and surrendering to Her, and by doing Liberation Breathing and Mantra Breathing, we are helping the planet. This is good karma for all of us!!

We want to avert catastrophe in our relationships, our bodies, our societies and our countries. How do we deal with the shadows in ourselves and in our societies? Logic cannot always find the answer, but the feminine side of ourselves is more capable of harmonizing the light and the shadows. Extraordinary changes do take place when the Goddess is accepted. That goes for women and men alike. I have interviewed many men whose lives were completely changed by surrendering to the Divine Mother. These men happen to be like saints.

(Mother Teresa said that your only regret at the end of your life should be that you did not become a saint.)

THINK ABOUT THAT.

We have not given attention to this aspect of God; partly because of the patriarchy and because of old beliefs that the Goddess is pagan and heathen. Both are incorrect.

If you want to really experience the Divine Mother, I go more thoroughly into this subject in my book, *Rock Your World with the Divine Mother*.

You can find it on Amazon here: bit.ly/MotherRay

Praise to you, Divine Mother. Make our lives a miracle. Show us what to do and how to do it. Let us be innocent and receptive like a child. Make our hearts Your temple. May people who read this receive Your wondrous grace and power.

Praise to you, Divine Mother. Make our lives a miracle. Show us what to do and how to do it. Let us be innocent and receptive like a child. Make our hearts your temple. May people who read this receive your wondrous grace and power.

WHO IS BABAJI?

Babaji, also named Sri Sri Bhagwan Herakhan Wale Baba, is an immortal Maha Avatar and yogi master. ("Avatar" means "descent of the Divine into matter.") Babaji is an emanation of Divine Light, Who, out of compassion, manifested in human form on earth by materializing a body. (In other words, in this incarnation, He was not born of a woman.) He is therefore the guru of the gurus. *He came to urge humanity to progress on the path of truth, simplicity, love and service to mankind.*

(That is His *formula for happiness*—did you take that in???)

Babaji is the power of the Eternal Father, Mother, and Divine Child. He can assume any form, any time He wishes, and can change that form at any time. In fulfillment of ancient scriptural and prophetic predictions, He materialized a youthful body in 1970 in a cave near the village of Hairakhan, in the Kumaon foothills of the Himalayas. He was accessible for 14 years on the last visit. He was and still is omnipresent. His form is limitless and beyond the scope of time. He is the essence of all religions and transcends every belief. He teaches through vibrations and direct experience in a way that words cannot express. To try to explain Him to you always seems inadequate.

I want you to know that if you are reading this book, He is available to you. He says: "My love is available, you can take it or not." I ask you: Why Not?? I had the great blessing to be with Him personally several times. I met Him in India three times and he actually materialized to me once right here in the USA. It is my humblest desire to share Him with you.

If you really want to be close to Him, and if you really want to go as high as possible, come with us to the Divine Mother Festival in India in the Spring.

Check out India Quest : bit.ly/IQRay

Try to imagine what it would be like for you to have both the Divine Mother and Babaji in your life. You deserve it!

LIBERATION BREATHING

The breath has incredible healing properties. When used in such a way that it is conscious, deep, and connected, the benefits are not only more oxygen, cleansing the cells of the body, but also greater energy of the life force (another name for the Divine Mother). Taking in greater life force cleanses the mind of its subconscious memories of hurts, anxiety, and conflict. By this method, you can be liberated from the following:

- ❖ Pain
- ❖ Negative thoughts
- ❖ Tension, or negative mental mass

- ❖ Shallow breathing
- ❖ Symptoms and disease
- ❖ Fear
- ❖ Anger
- ❖ Guilt
- ❖ Sadness
- ❖ The effects of traumatic incidents
- ❖ Blocks to abundance
- ❖ Addictions
- ❖ Negative patterns in relationships
- ❖ Birth Trauma
- ❖ Parental disapproval stuck in the mind
- ❖ Unconscious Death Urge
- ❖ The past, including past lives
- ❖ Depression
- ❖ The ego

You can use the breath to stabilize yourself / have more energy / enhance your immune system / create beneficial brain waves / travel to the interior of your being / acquire transcendent knowledge and information / and to seek higher consciousness.

Through our facilitation of thousands of sessions around the world, we regularly observe that Liberation Breathing results in:

- ❖ More bliss in daily life
- ❖ More pleasure in your physical body
- ❖ Increased physical energy
- ❖ Life becoming more effortless and fun
- ❖ The ability to breathe freely and naturally
- ❖ Work becoming more like play
- ❖ A dimension of spiritual energy which you may not have ever experienced
- ❖ The ability to receive love and have the direct experience of letting it in
- ❖ Increased psychic awareness

- ❖ More experience of telepathy and intuitive knowledge
- ❖ Transformations in physical appearance and beauty
- ❖ A propensity for youthfulness and desire for longevity
- ❖ Improved prosperity (Letting go of "there is not enough" mentality)
- ❖ Enhanced creative ability
- ❖ Greater personal connection to infinite intelligence.
- ❖ Seeing the truth about your hang-ups and ways to clear them
- ❖ Rising Self-Esteem

Would you not want all this to be available to you?

You can see why we make this our life long spiritual path.

If you don't have a spiritual path right now, this is for you. If you already have one, this will add to it.

Markus and I are available for private sessions here: bit.ly/LBSession

You can learn to give yourself sessions of Mantra Breathing however it is crucial that you have at least one session with us to train your breath mechanism correctly.

When we are doing Liberation Breathing, we are opening up to God, especially to the Divine Mother.

When one does this deep breathing, and there is discomfort, one must be sure to let go of the thought, "I can't get out of this discomfort." If one keeps breathing, it will go out. Just say, "I turn over this fear of discomfort to the Holy Spirit."

The Holy Spirit is the action of the Divine Mother. It is like the "gas" that is in the car. Without it, the car goes nowhere.

When we are
doing Liberation
Breathing,
we are opening
up to God,
especially
to the Divine
Mother.

Shaking is okay in breathwork, as long as it is spontaneous and not forced by one's will. But it is imperative to keep doing deep breathing while the shaking is going on.

While breathing, one can say, "I am letting go. The Divine Mother is healing me and blessing me."

**Spiritual workouts:

   a. Breathe in silence
   b. Breathe to Mantras for one hour
   c. Breathe underwater.

Liberation Breathing is a breathing meditation. It is better than regular meditation because anything negative coming up can be breathed out on the spot.

One can try breathing for 15 minutes while just saying, "Thank you," in one's mind. Very powerful. Imagine on the inhale one says, "Thank," and on the exhale, "you." Pull the energy up from inside and join it with the Dream Team and then send it down to someone on the exhale.

We should BREATHE OUT anything that is not our Real Self.

When releasing fear, one should never skip the Liberation Breathing.

On the inhale, take in God.
On the exhale, let go of the ego.

MANTRA BREATHING

A mantra is a powerful sound vibration that you can use to get into a deep spiritual state. It is the basis of all religions, traditions and scriptures. Repeating a mantra is a wonderful pleasing spiritual practice!

These mantras, which are sometimes chanted, are for expressing our love to our Guru or God. The best thing we could ever do is sing praises to God or the Guru. That will heal us. Mantras are the highest thoughts.

It does not matter if we understand a Sanskrit mantra or not. Listening to it, the meaning goes into us anyway.

I am going to now tell you all the possible benefits of working with mantras while practicing Liberation Breathing, which is "Mantra Breathing."

Liberation Breathing is the Divine Mother's Gift to us—deep, circular, connected energy breathing with no holding at the top of the inhale, and no holding at the bottom of the exhale.

We listen to the mantras being chanted while lying down breathing—connecting a deep inhale with a deep exhale in the upper chest.

Pull the breath up to the throat chakra and envision it going even above the head; then relax and let go, envisioning the exhale falling down through all the chakras, even to the bottom of root chakra. Then begin the pulling upwards again.

Keep this circular, smooth rhythm going. No pause at the top and no pause at the bottom. The energy will build.

Once you have that breathing rhythm going, direct your mind to the mantra.

When listening to the mantra, we must try to stay focused on the words—the sounds of them in your head. If the mind wanders, that is ok. Just bring it back.

Perhaps the mantra is pushing up old thoughts and this is good.

But we must try to go back to focusing on the mantra and get it in our head while it is playing. We must act as if we were singing it.

Deep breathing while listening to the mantra will help us let go of troubling memories and past incidents.

Listening to, or singing the mantra, will heal us. We can sing the mantra, but it is very, very beneficial to do Liberation Breathing while taking in the manta. That is a double-whammy.

To be closer to God, meditate and breathe with the following mantras:

Ocean of Devotion by Goma
River of Grace by Goma
Sacred Source by Goma.

Here is a Bahjan from "River of Grace" on YouTube: https://bit.ly/GOMA-1

Or you can also get other very wonderful mantras off of YouTube. "Om Namaha Shivaya" is the main one that Babaji gave us to use.

He said this mantra is "more powerful than the atomic bomb."

Imagine the mantra going into one's body while focusing on the Dream Team.

This is the "ultimate spiritual bath!"

When we are afraid it is a good time to play the mantras.

One should even try to have a massage to the mantras.

Doing the mantra "Om Namaha Shivaya" will save us.

One can take the mantra in one's hands and then move the hands over an affected part of the body where there is a symptom. Imagine putting the mantra in that part of the body with your hands.

Place the hands on the body and often think: "I put God here."

While doing mantra breathing try saying in your mind, "I let in the light."

The mantra can push out tension. Even if you fall asleep, the mantra will keep working on you. But you will get more healing if you stay conscious and repeat it in your mind while deep breathing.

To be closer to God, meditate and breathe with the following mantras which are the best: I am going to give you the advantage of each one.

Ocean of Devotion by Goma: You will immerse yourself in the mantra, "Om Namaha Shivaya," which Babaji says is the highest thought.

Sacred Source by Goma: There are more mantras here to the Divine Mother. In India they say there is nothing higher than worship of the Divine Mother.

River of Grace by Goma: The music behind the mantras is stronger here. It helps the mantra go in. There is also the sound of the water—the river in Herakhan—it is cleansing.

Start with *Ocean of Devotion*, because then you will fall in love with "Om Namaha Shivaya," which Babaji says is the highest thought. The other mantras are excellent also—different sounds are good as they reach different parts of the body.

Playing it quite loud is good so you can let it take over more that way.

Imagine the mantra going into the body while focusing on the "Dream Team" (Babaji, Jesus of ACIM and the Divine Mother).

It is even better to listen to Goma with the headphones and consistently notice how the joy of the music feels in the body.

The mantra will help take out the past as long as you are willing; and that also depends on how much you can concentrate on it and how deeply you breathe. You can replace the past with the mantra, *which is God.*

You can get good ideas while listening to the mantra. Have a writing pad nearby.

If we take in the mantra by breathing deeply into it, the mantra will push out our tension.

In the silence, after the mantra is finished playing, we feel a lot closer to God as the mantra brought us there.

As we listen to Goma with headphones we can consistently notice how our body begins to feel better.

The mantra will help take out the past as long as one is willing.

One can replace the past with the mantra.

When listening to the mantra, focus on the SOUND, and your BREATHING.

You can get good ideas while listening to the mantra. Have a writing pad nearby.

We can imagine the mantras going to the Divine Mother and She receives them and sends blessings down to help us relax.

During the mantra, place hands on any discomfort in your body and say, "I put God here."

The slower mantras can be used for relaxation. The faster ones can be used to clear something.

After listening to the mantra and breathing to it for an hour, lie still in the silence and feel the clear energy in the room and soak it in.

The minute I put the mantra where the discomfort is, the Divine Mother starts the blessing and the healing that area in my body.

We can imagine the mantras going to the Divine Mother and She receives them and sends blessings down to help us relax.

The mantra is bringing to you the love of God.

The mantras have a real healing power. Take advantage of that and stay focused on God. The mantra can solve all your problems as listening to it is pushing out all your blocks.

The mantra is everything. Liberation Breathing is everything. Together they are more of everything!!

You are going to FEEL BETTER if you can hold the mantra in your mind.

You don't want to miss out from the JOY of the mantra by letting yourself get distracted.

Imagine HOLDING the mantra in your mind and don't let it escape. If you listen carefully to it and stay conscious without your mind wandering, you will then have it as if you are singing it yourself. That is your praise. That is what will work.

IMAGINE YOUR HEART OPENING UP DURING THE MANTRA.

The Divine Mother mantras are handling everything.

The mantra will not only heal you, it will make you more alive and more happy. When you do Mantra Breathing, you are taking God in the body.

The mantra will get you to your perfection.

The mantra will make you stronger.

The mantra pushes fear out of the body.

You can learn better with the mantra as you are more connected to Infinite Intelligence.

If ever you see something very troubling, start to do the mantra immediately to cancel out any traumatic stress.

The mantra can clear your mind. It can repair your body.

The mantra leads your mind to what is important.

The mantra is a very high frequency. That is why the above is true.

The mantra is God in action.

The mantra is the opposite of mass shootings. The mantra is SANITY!

The mantra will help alter your bad habits and addictions.

Get to the point where you really, really feel this: "I am breathing this mantra into my body. It is taking over my body."

Move your hands in a special way, putting the mantra into any stuck or affected parts of the body.

The mantra will energize your INTENTION.

The mantra will energize and access spiritually high states of consciousness. Fill your mind with the Love of God through reciting the mantra.

Your True Mind holds only what you think with God, and I assure you the mantra is a Thought of God.

The mantra is also your highest thought that will bring you your best results in life. Why would you not want to breathe into that?

The Dream Team gives us very high thoughts that can all become our mantras. Start with "Om Namaha Shivaya" and build up from there. "I am the perfect love of God," is also a mantra. Use these two and get going.

God is more
Help with
Everything.

God wants to
make our
Whole life
Perfect.

Happiness is
God's goal
For us.

Every moment can be a Celebration.

Every moment is a highlight.

There is Something great coming.

ADDITIONS

Food for Thought

It is a good idea for you to learn to stay relaxed no matter what is going on.

It is a good idea to write down all your fears about the world crisis and share them with someone and then breathe them out.

It is a good idea to remember that we signed up for this situation.

It is a very smart idea to allow God's love to overtake all fears.

It is a good idea to focus on what is going to be your part in creating peace.

It is important to want to know what God is. It is important to want to feel what God is.

It is crucial to give up ALL fear—past, present and future.

It is very crucial to allow yourself to receive the Gifts of God:

- ❖ Peace
- ❖ Happiness
- ❖ A quiet mind
- ❖ A certainty of purpose
- ❖ A sense of worth and beauty that transcends the world
- ❖ Care
- ❖ Safety
- ❖ The warmth of sure protection always

- ❖ A quietness that cannot be disturbed
- ❖ A gentleness that can never be hurt
- ❖ A deep abiding comfort
- ❖ A rest so perfect that it can never be upset

Try to imagine having fun with God. That is totally possible.

It is possible to be free of all pain and discomfort. It is even possible to feel good all the time (but you must purify yourself for this to be your reality).

You have to be careful not to create a bad thing happening by worrying that it might happen (like a so called "inheritable disease" for example).

God is saying "I am here with you."

Let God's presence take you over.

It is important to consciously replace the fear in yourself with God's love.

To have a perfect body with no ailments, you have to get that you are perfect. This may be going against your religion as you might have been told only God is perfect. But of course, you ARE one with God so you are perfect.

You might not be letting the Holy Spirit take all your fear because you may have a fear of giving up fear, and you may have a doubt that the Holy Spirit could do that. (But Jesus of ACIM would not lie to you!)

Letting go, relaxing, and feeling safe, all go together. The more relaxed you are the safer you are. The opposite of being relaxed would be holding on to fear, guilt and anger—all of which cause tension and are defenses. Defenses attract attack so then how could you even be relaxed?

Letting go, relaxing and feeling safe all go together.

When you completely let go you hear God.

If you don't find your way (your mission), your way will be crooked!

If you have a problem, have fun with it.

Try to have fun with God!!

Why would you want to go over the past if you did not like it? That only keeps it!

When you are happier you can more easily avoid any addiction. Addictions are related to problems you made up. Problems are "games" you made up to have to clear yourself.

Don't make up an upset so you have an excuse to go back to your addiction.

Being filled with God is more relaxing than any medication.

The minute you go into fear, SNAP OUT OF IT! No fear equals the realm of miracles.

Give up the idea that power is dangerous. True Power is: Love / Safety / and Certainty.

Work is Worship

Try to ENJOY everything you are doing, even if it is a 9-5 job!

If you don't enjoy something you have to do, change your thoughts about doing it, OR, hire someone to do it for you.

You think you need something to be happy, but what you need to do is to be happy about everything.

If you surrender totally to being here, you will be relaxed.

When the fear is gone, it feels great to be here. Replace the fear with the love of God.

Listening to bird songs is good. That is the opposite of fear.

Formula for the very best life: "We are in the cave with Babaji and Jesus is living with us."

Doing beautiful things for people will make you feel good.

AFFIRMATIONS

These affirmations are obviously for me; however, I would be crazy not to share them with you. When you are reading, just imagine that each statement is for you.

I am letting go of anything that interferes with my perfection.

I accept my perfection and my perfection is now experienced in all areas of my life.

My perfection keeps my energy clear and people's dark energy away from me.

I am free of all guilt. I accept my natural innocence.

I am letting go of all doubt.

I am now relaxed at all times.

I am always innocent. Therefore, I don't unconsciously do things that make me feel guilty.

I completely respect myself, therefore others always respect me.

I have a natural shield of protection around me at all times.

Joy is my natural state now.

I am feeling really, really good, and I have a lot of energy.

I am feeling younger and more alive.

I feel my strength is increasing.

It is safe to give up suffering and experience my holiness instead.

There is a point where my peace just takes over. This peace always protects me.

I am also always protected by a pyramid of light around me.

When I realize that some people want to keep their errors and do not want to change, I can let go and not feel like I failed.

I know God loves me and wants to give me everything, so why not be open to receive it all?

I allow God to give me what He wants to give me!

There is zero anger between me and
_____, and zero anger between me
and anyone.

I feel joy within me now.

I enjoy consciously thinking good
thoughts.

Every time I think of my Guru, Babaji, I am
improving more.

My improvements are noticeable to me
and everyone.

I am willing for God to show me who I
really am. I completely let go of my false
self.

The area around my heart is opening up.
My rib cage is expanding.

The beauty of God is healing me.

God is restoring my sanity.

The more attracted I am to God, the better I feel.

People's anger melts in my presence.

God is exotic. God is mystical. God is interesting. God only gives.

Strength and relaxation go together. The more I am relaxed, the stronger I am.

I can lie here and be happy for no reason.

It is totally safe to be happy all the time.

I am 100% present with myself.

Everything is going to be just fine.

A plethora of joyful experiences is coming.

I am perfect and I am experiencing my perfection.

Every day in every way I feel better and better.

I am giving up all agony from all lifetimes. I forgive my entire past.

I can handle more and more happiness by doing my deep breathing sessions.

I no longer create any bad consequences for anything I do.

I receive happiness and I give happiness.

I am totally relaxed into more love.

I am doing this deep breathing so I feel good.

I am getting more and more sane and more and more safe as a result!

It feels really good to be here, therefore, I love being here.

I am a lightworker for my guru.

I choose to relax the rest of my life.

My light will help people raise up!

My love for myself heals me (and others too).

Formula for a great life: We are always in the cave with Babaji and Jesus lives with us.

Everything I do contributes to more joy in my life.

The happier I am being here, the better I feel. The better I feel, the happier I am being here.

The more of God I take in, the more relaxed I am.

People now want to be in my frequency. This thought increases my business.

Life is fun!

I am only going to have good thoughts now.

I am not going to judge anything.

I help everyone go to the next level of service. Everyone gets clear on their mission around me.

I am ready to experience my perfection in my body. My body is now in its state of perfection.

I am 100% relaxed.

I go to the next level of joy now. The more open I am to God, the more joy I feel. I keep opening up to God.

Others, therefore, feel really good around me.

My thoughts are getting higher and higher.

I AM perfection itself.

My Real Self has no fear. I want the state of no fear. I am aware of my Real Self.

The closer I am to God, the less fear I have. Divine Mother, I give you all my fear.

I allow Shiva (that part of God that destroys ignorance) to take out all my stuck-ness.

I can be here and be in Heaven as long as I stay focused on God.

I let the Divine Mother take this issue (negative situation) from me.

The more I clear my mind, the less tension I have.

I am doing great. I am healthy, happy and feeling good.

I give over to the Holy Spirit my fear of death and my habit of death over all lifetimes!

I want to be completely open to more of God.

I don't let my mistakes turn into upsets!

Oneness leads to rejuvenation!

I am flooded with high thoughts!

I give up all false idols.

I have Babaji's energy with me all day.

I am willing to have my FAITH totally restored.

I am becoming the best possible version of myself.

I am completely open to the new energy coming from Babaji. I let in the manna of the Divine Mother.

I am feeling good all the time now.

I am letting go totally. I know letting go leads to "letting in."

People get better and feel better after talking to me. Everyone goes away from me happier.

I am bringing in the energy of Babaji.

I do not take the negative people "out there," or the negative things into my consciousness.

When I take people to the Divine Mother, I am leading them to miracles. I can always get the right solution by going to the highest thought.

I am staying in the present while God is thrusting me ahead.

I stay in the present while I keep moving ahead. Even if I don't understand, I keep moving ahead. I keep doing the right thing.

I can now relax and stay relaxed. Something amazing is in my future!

I am in agreement with God, who is exceeding my expectations!!

The right people are tracking me down. My time is coming! I am receiving explosive blessings!! God is richly rewarding me.

I love my future!! In fact, I am enjoying each day more than the one before!!

AN INVITATION

Congratulations on getting this far with the book and finishing it! I hope that you will now consider having Babaji as your personal Master. People need a spiritual master. At a time like this when everything is in chaos, it is very helpful to have a spiritual master. Some people think if you have a guru or master, then you have to give your power away. Nothing could be farther from the truth. A true master helps you get into your own power and stand on your own feet. With a master guiding you, you are able to touch your own wholeness and perfection faster. What will make you really happy is experiencing who you really are. As you get closer to the Master, you will find more of your true self. The Master helps you dispel your ignorance, your limitations, your fears, your karma and your ego in general. Otherwise undoing your ego alone can be very hard to do.

So why not come to India with us to Babaji's ashram and get really connected to Him? We go every year in the Spring. The dates vary depending on the dates of Spring Navaratri—the "Divine Mother Festival."

Go here for more info: bit.ly/IQRay

ABOUT THE AUTHOR

SONDRA RAY, author of 29 books on the subjects of relationships, healing, and spiritual matters, was launched into international acclaim in the 1970s as one of the pioneers, along with Leonard Orr, of the Rebirthing Experience. She has trained thousands of people all over the world in this conscious connected breathwork process and is considered one of the foremost experts on how the birth trauma affects one's body, relationships, career, and life. As she puts it, "This dynamic breathing process produces extraordinary healing results in all of your relationships—with your mate, with yourself, and with Life—very fast. By taking in more Life Force through the breath, limiting thoughts and memories, which are the cause of all problems and disease, come to the surface of the mind so they can be 'breathed out', forgiven, and released."

Applying over 40 years of metaphysical study, she has helped thousands of people heal their negative thought structures, birth trauma, habitual family patterns, and unconscious death urge. She encourages people to make lasting positive changes through Liberation Breathing® to be more free, happy, and productive. No matter what Sondra Ray is doing, she is always trying to bring about a higher consciousness. Recently she has written new books on the subject of *Spiritual Intimacy©* and *BABAJI: My*

Miraculous Meetings with a Maha Avatar, and *Physical Immortality*, in which she envisions a shift in the current paradigm in relationships around the world to a new level of awareness—free from anger, conflict and even death.

OTHER RESOURCES

Sondra Ray / – author, teacher, Rebirther, creator of the Loving Relationships Training®, Co-founder of Liberation Breathing® and Quests to Sacred Sites around the world:

Facebook: www.facebook.com/sondra.ray.90

Facebook Fan Page:
www.facebook.com/LiberationBreathing

Twitter: www.twitter.com/SondraRay1008

YouTube: www.youtube.com/sondraray

Instagram: www.instagram/sondraray

Sondra Ray's Website: www.sondraray.com

Sondra Ray's Events: bit.ly/EventsRay

SONDRA RAY'S AUTHOR'S PORTAL

Bit.ly/SondraRay

BOOKS BY

SONDRA RAY &
MARKUS RAY

THE SUPERMARKET FOR A MEANINGFUL LIFE

In this storehouse of wisdom to navigate the Pandemic, Sondra Ray and Markus Ray give us a "supermarket" to fill our shopping cart full of ideas and interests to keep our ascension into more Pure Joy a reality. A Supermarket for a Meaningful Life helps supply you with the soul food you need to navigate these times—from a Look at Art, to tools for improving your relationships, and how to strengthen your Life Purpose. This is the book for coming out of this Pandemic spiritually well-nourished.

AMAZON LINK: getbook.at/Supermarket

THE SANCTUARY OF SILENCE

Markus Ray leads us on a journey to find the Peace and Quiet of a spiritual life inside of ourselves. He uses his every day encounters to demonstrate that the "Sanctuary of Silence" is within us. Art is discussed in the most poignant way, especially El Greco, in this sensual look at how daily experience is next to holiness.

AMAZON LINK: getbook.at/Sanctuary

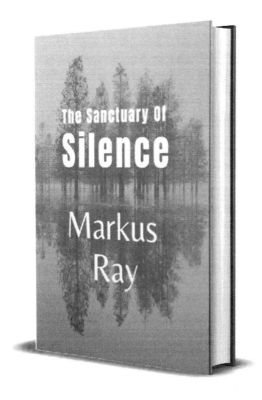

THE PERFECTION OF BABAJI

Sondra Ray tells more of her wild stories of encounters she had with her Life Teacher, Babaji. These little stories always make a point of a life lesson we all need to get. Come with her on these journeys into the Perfection of Babaji, from the perspective of a Western seeker who wants to get the ultimate benefit from having a Spiritual Master.

AMAZON LINK: www.bit.ly/PerfectionRay

LATELY I'VE BEEN THINKING II: POWERFUL POSTS FOR AN AWESOME LIFE 𝄞

Sondra Ray, continues to bring us her wisdom from Facebook with her daily posts written over a period of two years. This continuation of Spiritual and Relationships advice enlightens us on many common questions—from finding your life's purpose to discovering your formula for happiness. These 𝄞 posts for an awesome life are what we need in these times.

AMAZON LINK: www.bit.ly/Lately2Ray

LATELY I'VE BEEN THINKING: POWERFUL POSTS FOR AN AWESOME LIFE ⅁

Relationships expert and spiritual mentor, Sondra Ray, brings her wisdom to Facebook with daily posts written over a period of two years. These tidbits of advice uplift and enlighten us on many common life subjects—from finding your life's purpose to discovering your formula for happiness. Markus Ray, Sondra's twin flame, compiled these short entries to bring you these powerful ⅁ posts for an awesome life.

AMAZON LINK: www.bit.ly/LatelyRay

ALPHA OMEGA

In the companion to SONDRA RAY's *Lately I've Been Thinking*, Markus Ray compliments his wife's free flowing commentaries on Liberation Breathing / Breathwork, *A Course in Miracles*, Holy Relationships, and wisdom for day-to-day living. These guides for various Spiritual Quests to Sacred Sites around the world, continue their prolific output of written roadmaps to purposeful living.

AMAZON LINK: www.bit.ly/AORay

LIBERATION: FREEDOM FROM YOUR BIGGEST BLOCK TO PURE JOY

What is your biggest block to having Happiness all of the time? What's keeping you in a polite hell? Why has your life fallen short of Heaven on Earth? This book by Sondra Ray and Markus Ray will answer these questions for you, and provide the thread out of the labyrinth of your most negative thoughts in your subconscious that are sabotaging your life, or preventing you from going all the way to Pure Joy. Discover what they call a "Personal Lie," that is your most negative belief about yourself, hidden in the deep recesses of your psyche. Everyone has one to overcome. It is a main cause of all the things and events that went wrong in your life. Free yourself from it by reading this book, and practicing a few forgiveness processes.

AMAZON LINK: www.bit.ly/LibRay

THE MASTER IS BEAUTIFUL

THIS IS A BOOK for you to have holy relationships directly with Spiritual Masters in your life. Do you want them? Markus Ray presents 9 parts in this book, each dedicated to a Spiritual Master who has greatly contributed to the eternal Wisdom of human spiritual evolution. He makes these Masters and their messages very accessible to the general public, in a way that can endear them to anyone interested in transforming themselves "upward" in their process of enlightenment.

AMAZON LINK: www.bit.ly/MasterRay

I DESERVE LOVE

This book can clear up your sex life—totally—and infuse new Joy into your sensuality! You Deserve the Perfect Lover, and Sondra Ray tells you how to find and win that person. You need only decide what would make you completely happy in a relationship and you can achieve it, quickly and without struggle. The Power to get what you want is within you, and you can tap into it through the simple affirmations set forth in this dynamic book. Sondra Ray explains simply and clearly how to use the tested affirmations exercises, how to adapt them to your specific needs, and how to put them to immediate use. If it sounds too easy, read the many case histories that demonstrate their effectiveness. Then prove it to yourself—put affirmations to work in your own life!

AMAZON LINK: www.bit.ly/DeserveRay

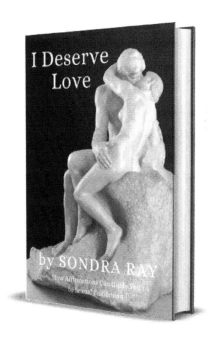

PHYSICAL IMMORTALITY: HOW TO OVERCOME DEATH

This is a book that can permanently lift you out of despair, depression and hopelessness—a book that shows you how longevity is the linear result of quantum living.

Sondra Ray teaches you how to dismantle the unconscious and hypnotic program (the unconscious death urge) which is literally killing you. The real tragedy of the unconscious death urge is not only that it causes us to die before our time, but that it generates a resistance-to-life of pure JOY. It makes life less attractive and therefore intensifies our desire to die and put an end to our misery. It's a vicious cycle. This book is the solution that is 100% affirmative of life that offers a viable alternative.

AMAZON LINK: www.bit.ly/ImmortalRay

THE NEW LOVING RELATIONSHIPS BOOK

Working through the depths of self-awareness using affirmations and emotional exercises, this book shows that loving relationships begin with self-love. Ray demonstrates how to find, achieve, and maintain deeper, more fulfilling relationships.

Revitalize what it means to be in a Loving Relationship. Save decades of time and get clear that you deserve Pure Joy ! Get the basics, which are all the beatitudes of gratitude that take you higher and higher in your Love together.

AMAZON LINK: www.bit.ly/NLRBRay

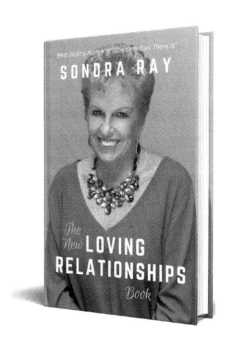

BABAJI: MY MIRACULOUS MEETINGS WITH A MAHA AVATAR

This book may just blow you mind. The wild stories of a wild woman meeting her wild Guru in 1977, and all the stories of subsequent meetings afterwards. Unbelievable and true—off the charts encounters with Babaji, the Maha Avatar first mentioned in Yogananda's Autobiography of a Yogi in chapters 33 & 34—but in real life, in real time with Sondra Ray.

You can know Him. This book is about Him. He says to you, "My Love is available. You can take it or not." Why not take it?

AMAZON LINK: www.bit.ly/BabajiRay

SPIRITUAL INTIMACY: WHAT YOU REALLY WANT WITH A MATE

What people really want in their relationships is deep connection, good communication, and spiritual intimacy. Sondra Ray and Markus Ray explore these common desires. They also give you 18 good ingredients that establish spiritual intimacy. And these ingredients permeate into all areas of your life, and transform them to embody truth, simplicity and love throughout.

AMAZON LINK: www.bit.ly/IntimacyRay

ODES TO THE DIVINE MOTHER

Through intimate portraits and inspired meditations, Markus Ray cracks open the sacredness in coffee cups, mountaintops, airports, and vistas to reveal a Source that is divinely feminine. Infused with the essence of his lifelong study of *A Course in Miracles*, each page explores topics from ego and forgiveness to joy, Holy relationships, and Christ consciousness through daily dialogue with the Divine Mother. A sacred stillness emerges as one's consciousness opens—line by line to the purity, power, love, and perfection that is the Divine Feminine.

AMAZON LINK: www.bit.ly/OdesRay

LITTLE GANESH BOOK

Solve all you problems with this book! In this collection of short aphorisms and meditations, Markus Ray pays homage to Ganesh—the Elephant God in Eastern mythology Who is the remover of obstacles. You can use them to inspire your day, and to remove the difficult hurdles in your own life.

AMAZON LINK: www.bit.ly/GaneshRay

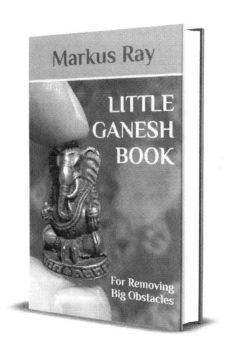

LIBERATION BREATHING: THE DIVINE MOTHER'S GIFT

This is Sondra Ray's "Bible on Breathwork"—a guidebook for expanding into life, spirit, and happiness through the power of your own breath. Discover how Liberation Breathing — a form of breathwork practiced worldwide—transforms on the mental, physical, and spiritual dimensions. Sondra Ray's newest book on Breathwork elevates the soul while releasing readers from negative thoughts, traumas, and relationship patterns. Ray unites the power of breath with her extraordinary commitment to healing and miracles as she details the evolution of Liberation Breathing.

AMAZON LINK: www.bit.ly/LiberationRay

MIRACLES WITH MY MASTER, TARA SINGH

In this book, author MARKUS RAY comes forward to transmit to you the many blessings he received from his teacher of "A Course in Miracles," TARA SINGH. This touching story of miracles, raising the dead, meeting the saints of India is compellingly and openly told within. MARKUS spent seventeen years studying with TARA SINGH from Easter of 1989 to March of 2006 , and describes him as, "my life teacher, my spiritual guide, my Master, and my friend."

AMAZON LINK: www.bit.ly/TSRay

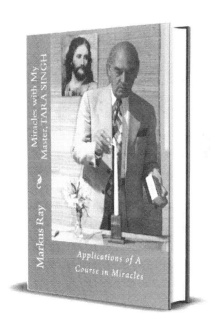

ROCK YOUR WORLD WITH THE DIVINE MOTHER

"Those who explored the frontiers of universal spiritual consciousness were true pioneers. Their ideas were mind blowing and life altering for an entire generation, for whom such beliefs were startlingly outside the box. One of those pioneers was Sondra Ray.... If Sondra writes a new book, I read it. I let go of my left brain and drink her in, imagining her sitting on a chair, explaining to me what to her is so obvious and the rest of us, well, maybe not so much. I have never experienced Sondra as anything other than a beam of light.... I have lived enough to be able to say that of all the good fortunes I have had in my life, encountering her has been one of the liveliest. Sondra Ray is more than a woman.....The word GODDESS comes to mind...." — Marianne Williamson—

AMAZON LINK: www.bit.ly/MotherRay

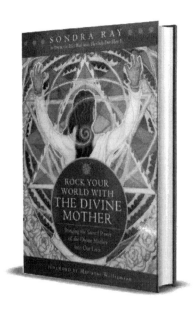

PELE'S WISH

"Pele's Wish continues the bold, wonderful saga of Sondra Ray's journey into Spirit. She makes everything we long for seem so possible. We are very lucky to have her in our midst." —Marianne Williamson—

AMAZON LINK: www.bit.ly/PeleRay

HEALING AND HOLINESS

Are you going through a rough time? Or are you are concerned about someone in crisis in your life? This book is for you. Respected author, teacher, and nurse turned metaphysical healer Sondra Ray shares her spiritual and physical journey in HEALING AND HOLINESS. Written as an intimate personal testimony, Sondra tells of her struggles-toiling through difficult exercises with her spiritual masters—and her triumphs—experiencing the transformative powers of rebirthing and metaphysical healing—as she learns to recondition her mind and body to heal with and without using Western medicine. Originally released under the title HEALING WITH SONDRA RAY, this edition offers new insight into the workings of the unconscious mind and our ability to affect the way the mind controls the body. HEALING AND HOLINESS is destined to become one of Sondra Ray's most important and beloved books.

AMAZON LINK: www.bit.ly/HolinessRay

THE LOVING RELATIONSHIPS TREASURY

Collected from her groundbreaking series of relationship books, THE LOVING RELATIONSHIPS TREASURY distills the core teachings of Sondra Ray's unique approach to finding, achieving, and maintaining the deepest, most fulfilling relationships possible. Ray's timeless writing continues to inspire us to begin our personal journeys toward integrating intimacy and spirituality within every significant relationship—with ourselves, our mates, our parents, our children, our colleagues, our world.

AMAZON LINK: www.bit.lyTreasuryRay

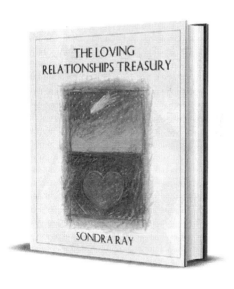

ESSAYS ON CREATING SACRED RELATIONSHIPS

CREATING SACRED RELATIONSHIPS is as much an intimate look at the woman behind the teaching as it is the culmination of her most recent spiritual initiations and encounters. Sondra Ray's riveting personal story is presented along with a collection of essays that inform, inspire, and promote the conscious exploration of new means and methods by which we may journey towards new relationships with ourselves, our mates, our business associates—our world. This gathering of thoughts explores nothing less than the creation of a new model for all our relationships. And this model is a manifestation of our own personal "heaven on earth."

AMAZON LINK: www.bit.ly/EssaysRay

INTERLUDES WITH THE GODS

In this account of Spiritual Masters who touched and shaped her life, Sondra Ray gives us a glimpse of some of the most off the chart meetings and impressions of these Holy Beings who represent the top shelf of human evolution. The list is not exhaustive by any means, but her descriptions of God-Like Beings she has met in her life gives us a kind of litmus test to find our own pantheon of enlightened beings to guide us as well. Writing in her crystal-clear vernacular style, Sondra gives us a blessing—a simple stroke of a divine caress in these various "Interludes with the Gods."

AMAZON LINK: www.bit.ly/InterludesRay

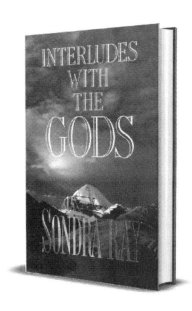

INNER COMMUNION

Here the author of Loving Relationships shares her special insights about the importance of spiritual nourishment of the self and one's relationships—the inner communion that can be achieved by opening up to the lessons of life and love. The finer nuances of spiritual nourishment are explored here in Sondra Ray's inspiring look at "communion." Nurturing ourselves through the experience of inner spiritual states leads us to richer relationships with ourselves, with others, and with God. Personal and touching, this book looks at communion from many aspects—from the strictly religious to the broader communion of intimate relationships and our place in the fabric of being.

AMAZON LINK: www.bit.ly/CommunionRay

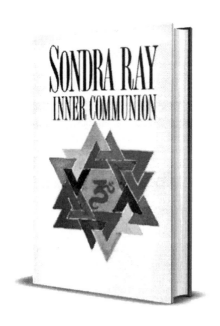

HOW TO BE CHIC, FABULOUS AND LIVE FOREVER

Sondra Ray's first book that considers the possibility of immortality, argues that one should be the most important, celebrated, and fashionable person in one's life, and tells how to take advantage of all life has to offer.

AMAZON LINK: www.bit.ly/FabulousRay

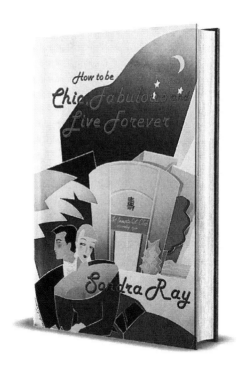

PURE JOY

Life can be filled with Pure Joy and Love, and there are many
spiritual practices, thoughts, and sacred texts to help us find
that joy. Here the author of *Loving Relationships* and *The Only
Diet There Is* shares her discoveries of the many spiritual
practices available to help us in our ascension upward on our
life journey— practices learned during Sondra's life-long
spiritual quest and leadership, and on her incredible spiritual
Quests to India and beyond.

AMAZON LINK: www.bit.ly/PureRay

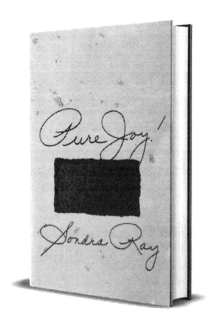

BIRTH AND RELATIONSHIPS

Did you ever think the circumstances at your birth could affect the rest of your life? Did you ever wonder if being induced made you not trust authority? Does difficulty completing things relate to being a cesarean delivery? Do you do things backwards because you were breech coming out of the womb? These are questions Sondra Ray asks and answers in this groundbreaking work on how your birth script affects your life and relationships.

AMAZON LINK: www.bit.ly/BirthRay

IDEAL BIRTH

Sondra Ray lays out the truth about giving birth, and takes the courageous road to introduce birthing practices that are enlightened—namely, underwater birth. She fills in the blanks and takes the mystique out of what should be a natural celebration and easy transition—not a "traumatic labor." This book will break the whole mindset of the medical model that grips women into a fear based and primarily patriarchal leftover from the days of Kings and male dominated obstetrics.

AMAZON LINK: www.bit.ly/IdealRay

DRINKING THE DIVINE

This book is for people interested in, or studying "A Course In Miracles." ACIM is a magnificent spiritual work that has brought many people to inner peace. "Drinking The Divine" provides a beautiful summary of the key points in the text section of ACIM.

AMAZON LINK: www.bit.ly/DrinkingRay

CELEBRATION OF BREATH

In this second primer on Rebirthing, Sondra Ray further elaborates on the effectiveness of Breathwork to change your life for the better. Basically, this book introduces people to the process of deep, circular connected energy breathing, in order to release stored subconscious memories that are hanging us up in life. This book discusses how to have well-being, physical perfection, healing and longevity by using Rebirthing/Breathwork.

AMAZON LINK: www.bit.ly/CelebrationRay

THE ONLY DIET THERE IS

Here is a book to change your life. It is a method for losing weight through positive thinking and the changing of attitudes toward life and food. Sondra Ray This, of course, is no ordinary 'diet' book...This is an extraordinary approach to weight loss—a diet of forgiveness, a fast from negative thought—and if followed one can achieve bodily perfection.

AMAZON LINK: www.bit.ly/DietRay

LOVING RELATIONSHIPS I

This easy to read book uses ideas and philosophies from Werner Erhard's EST training, Ernest Holmes' Religious Science, Rebirthing, Affirmations, as well as cognitive and traditional modes of psychotherapy to give the reader new insights into the nature of love relationships.

AMAZON LINK: bit.ly/LovingRay1

LOVING RELATIONSHIPS II

In LOVING RELATIONSHIPS II, Sondra Ray continues the journey she began with the publication of LOVING RELATIONSHIPS I in 1980. This entirely new book shares her discoveries and adventures as she investigates deeper into the secrets of love, life, and spirituality.

AMAZON LINK: bit.ly/LovingRay2

REBIRTHING IN THE NEW AGE

Co-authored with Leonard Orr, this was Sondra Ray's first "manual" for the process of Rebirthing—the conscious, connected circular energy breathing that was innovated by Leonard and her in the early 1970's in San Francisco. The clearing of negative subconscious memories all the way back to a person's birth through this deep "breathwork" is first clarified in this book.

AMAZON LINK: www.bit.ly/RebirthingRay

I DESERVE LOVE (First Edition)

This is the first book Sondra Ray published back in 1976. It is a classic book on the New Thought Movement, one of the first of its kind that made it clear that thoughts and feelings precede and determine all experiences. Before "Affirmations" was a household word, Sondra Ray wrote—*I Deserve Love.*

AMAZON LINK: www.bit.ly/IDeserveLove

NOTES

NOTES

Printed in Great Britain
by Amazon

7e0f53f2-9a63-4416-a95a-58c04542f7e1R01